AGILE
-ISH

How to create a culture of agility

Lynne Cazaly

Agile-ish

First published in 2017
Copyright © 2017 Lynne Cazaly
www.lynnecazaly.com

National Library of Australia Cataloguing-in-Publication entry:
Author: Lynne Cazaly, 1964 -
Title: Agile-ish: How to create a culture of agility
ISBN: 978-0-9874629-9-2

Subjects: Leadership.
                 Agile.
                 Change.
                 Teams.
                 Innovation.
                 Creativity.
                 Collaboration.
                 Communication.

Cover design by Lliam Amor
Hand drawn headings font by Lynne Cazaly

AGILE
-ISH

How to create a culture of agility
Lynne Cazaly

Agile-ish

Contents

Agile-ish

Behind the cover

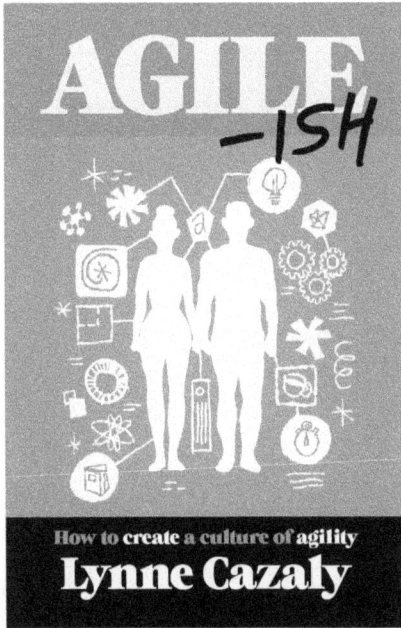

Many thanks to Lliam Amor for yet another of his cleverly creative cover designs.

Running from my often shallow or vague brief, Lliam is always able to hit on delightful and inspiring design elements.

He's designed the covers of each of my five books and this one brought back a few school days memories!

It looked part school textbook, part biology or science exercise book and even looked like it had been tampered or graffiti-ed by a student deep in a learning moment.

With those icons, the humans at the centre - the people who make things happen - this was very agile-ish indeed! It hit on the themes of hypothesis, testing, learning, a-ha moments and included scribbles and doodles of insight.

After all, this agile-ish thing is about people, ideas, experiments, learning and improvement.

Three cheers to you good man - thank you Lliam Amor!

Agile-ish

Hello

This is a book about agile. Ish. It's not really for people or businesses or teams who are already agile. In the agile community there is often a sense of 'you're agile or you're not' so yes, I'm publishing something that is somewhere in the middle-ish.

This is ideal for people, teams and organisations who want to begin or who are on the path or journey to being agile.

Being. Not doing. This is a clear distinction. We're gonna be. Not do. Agile. Ish.

Agile-ish is not the end game, the destination or the end result. It's the process, the journey. You're on your way to agile. So you are something in the meantime. What is it and how do you know when you are there anyway? And is it even something or somewhere you get to... and then stop? And who decides or deems or judges where you are up to?

Get started on the journey or path to agile. And in the meantime you will be agile-ish. Not agile yet. Not yet agile. What if it takes you three years or 12 years to get there? Or if you never get 'there'?

Go for it. Carry on. In the meantime you are doing fine and you are agile-ish.

These are my thoughts, insights, essays and posts on agile related topics.

Yours in transitions, journeys, paths and transformations. Carry on. Keep going.

Lynne.

'We need to be more agile'

Plenty of business leaders, conference speakers and even politicians are talking about 'agility' or being 'agile' in business.

You'll hear them say 'we need to be more agile' or 'it's all about agility'. Heck, even my very own Australian Prime Minster, Malcolm Turnbull said: *'The Australia of the future has to be a nation that is agile, that is innovative, that is creative.'*

Apart from cheetahs, jaguars and other agile animals able to move quickly and easily over land hunting prey, what's agile got to do with business?

Agile means quick, easy and nimble. In business it's a way of thinking, a way of working that is increasingly part of how many of the most successful companies work.

Born from the world of software project development, an agile team divides up work to be done so it can be completed quickly, easily and released to the market frequently. Quick, easy, nimble.

With the rise of apps on your mobile, the power of the internet and advances in technology, many businesses leverage technology to deliver services to their customers; the sooner they can deliver that service or the better that service is, the greater the value is for customers.

Getting great things into your customer's hands quickly is kind of what it's all about.

Beyond technology, other global changes demand agility: challenges from competitors, customer demands and government changes all mean the most adaptive, those who can change swiftly will survive, thrive and win.

There are casualties on the list of companies that didn't – or weren't and still aren't - changing quickly enough: Kodak,

Napster, Netscape, Blockbuster, Nokia, Yahoo... and many more sliding from Top 500 lists around the world.

In most cases they didn't adapt or change swiftly enough. They were slow, rigid and too stuck in their ways.

The path to being agile isn't travelled overnight. It takes time. Rather than complaining and wishing for 'the good old days' to return, adopting an agile frame of mind and being willing to adapt to changing conditions is what success is made of in today's world.

So some questions for you:

- In terms of mindset, how open are you to change... to really change things up?

- What changes are you noticing in your industry or your client's industry?

- What other businesses are you noticing adapt and change in their quest towards agility?

- Which parts of your business or practice could be stuck, rigid or too slow to adapt?

- Are you up for this?

Learning from techs, geeks and nerds

All the talk about agile and agility in business creates plenty of interest and claims that perhaps it's a fad or a cliché... but there is substance and history to the success of agile in business.

Where did this idea or way of working come from?

Agile began in the software development field – yes, those apps on your phone and the websites you interact with have in many cases been designed, developed, tested and delivered using an agile approach.

While hints at some of the elements of agile have been found in the 1950s onward, it was in 2001 that a group of software developers got together and created the landmark 'Manifesto for Software Development'.

The Agile Manifesto has served as a real beacon for software development – and increasingly other fields too - to help teams and organisations focus on the things that matter.

Things like:

- customer collaboration
- self-organising teams
- satisfying the customer
- face-to-face communication
- welcoming changes, even late in the process

are just part of the manifesto of four values and 12 principles.

You could see why 20 years ago this was considered innovative and progressive yet today, so many more businesses adopt these ways of thinking and working as their standard ways of working -- their survival depends on it!

Big name companies like Google, Spotify, Amazon, Salesforce, Cisco, Intuit and Microsoft have for many years had agile as part of how they think.

A-ha, this customer at the centre of things works. Who'd have thought! Techs, geeks and nerds are smart. They were on to this collaborative, communicative and iterative way of working before it was a 'thing'!

I find it clever that even though techs, geeks and nerds are making incredibly hi-tech applications, platforms and software systems, they tend to use more analogue, handcrafted and truly human ways of working. Collaboration, communication, transparency, conversations and feedback. This stuff works.

Increasingly hot on the heels of the tech giants using agile are financial institutions like ING, Rabobank, Commonwealth Bank and Westpac who have adopted agile as a way of thinking too.

Recently the CEO of Australia's ANZ Bank, Shayne Elliott said he would be slashing the bank's hierarchies and rigid structure to create a more agile environment just like the Agile Manifesto outlines.

Beyond their technical skills, techs, geeks and nerds know something! Agile isn't a fad; it's a very cool way of creating and delivering incredible value to customers.

Growing in adoption

Agile is more than a fad and it's intriguing to see how it grows in interest and adoption.

An agile mindset is about adapting, responding and iterating your services or products - to deliver value to your customer.

Agile has been synonymous with technology and software development projects. But it isn't limited to technology. Lots of other fields and teams use agile as a way to run their projects.

For some organisations, it might start with the Information Technology department, but then it grows. Other departments are often curious to see how the IT team is working and delivering things of value to customers quickly.

Human Resources

In Human Resources, there's been an HR Manifesto created not dissimilar to the Agile Manifesto. HR aims to build engaged workforces, thriving cultures and to help organisations and their leaders better respond to change.

Marketing

Marketers find they can gather data and develop solutions in real time. They can deploy tests quickly, evaluate the results and then rapidly iterate. You could imagine them having lots of different campaigns running at once with new ideas raised and then swiftly launched and tested continuously.

Schools and Education

A movement in education to become more agile is not just about how learning is designed and delivered by teaching teams, but how students can work on projects in their subjects in class. That's agile within an agile environment!

Design, Legal, Finance ... have also brought agile to the way they think and work.

There are examples of agile working in manufacturing, aviation, broadcasting and... I spoke with a winery recently about how they could be more agile in how they respond, adapt and iterate from the grape to the bottle and beyond. Cheers!

Whatever the industry, if things are complex, uncertain or changing rapidly, it's worth looking at how you can bring agility to the way things get done.

Customers increasingly want instant products and services and you can't deliver those using the same old bureaucracy your industry's been using for the past century. You have to become more nimble, more agile if you're going to respond and adapt.

This isn't just about being more productive or getting more work done; it's actually about getting more value out of the work you're doing – so yes, it's smarter not harder.

As some of the team from Microsoft say, *'if you have an idea, how quickly can you get that idea out of your head and into the customer's hands?'*

This is agile.

It's even happening in Formula 1 motor racing. I loved this description of competitive and competition in the sport in Patrick Collister's book *'How to use innovation and creativity in the workplace'*. He explains how adaptive, responsive and competitive Formula 1 racing can be:

'When you compete, you are a participant. To be a competitor, you have to adapt and change. Our speed of development is mind-blowing. In season, we are making a new component, designed, developed and manufactured and going onto the car every 12 and a half minutes.

This is agile-ish.

Something needs changing

Yes, yes the world is changing and so too must we -- and our teams and businesses.

We need to respond to disruption. But while doing that, we can also make an attempt at reducing the risk of the large-scale, slow moving projects that take an eternity to 'roll out' through a business. What if at the end of that project no one wants it, buys it, needs it or... or potentially worse... it doesn't work?

Rather, we need to be building a culture of experimentation so that success is easier, quicker and more enjoyable and exciting to attain.

Most leaders and their teams when quizzed would say that something needs to change. The lowest engagement scores, the unhappiest of teams, the highest of turnovers, the highest levels of stress, whispers and bullying, sexist, racist and unfriendly workplaces - somethin' needs a'changing. Quick.

I see a place where we can be using the principles or ideas of agile yet not be orthodox or pure or 100% complete and total or proper about agile. There is a demand for the elements, characteristics and ways of thinking and working that agile has proven. Let's borrow from that.

By working in agile-like ways, we strengthen our agility; we'll be more able to adapt because we will be adapting.

Being agile-ish, thinking agile-ish will give us the ability to increase commitment, be sharper in decision making and help us handle the VUCA (volatility, uncertainty, complexity and ambiguity) of the world which isn't going away anytime soon.

ISH

Agile-ish

22

What's with 'ish'?

Let's get this sorted.

Yes I could have written a book titled 'Agile'.

But I'm an 'ish' kind of person.

'Ish' means that it's not perfect, it's not perfectly done but it's out there.

It's version one!

'Ish' means somewhat.

It mean reasonably or fairly.

Most of all... it means more or less.

To a degree. Or a part.

Something. Or other.

To a small degree. Or to an extent.

Ish is not finished or done or complete or perfect.

It's the opposite. It's in progress, underway and wonderfully imperfect.

Ish is not broken or stalled or stopped or undone or half-baked or problematic.

Ish is about being in progress or underway.

It's happening. If you want it now it won't be fully done it will be somewhat. Part of it will be done.

I like the ish-ness of many aspects of life.

When you're going to meet up with someone and they ask you, *'What time do you want to meet up?'* and you might reply, *'How about six-ish?'*

It means give or take a few minutes. It means you're open to meeting up a bit later (or earlier).

For those among us who call ourselves perfectionists - or use this as a reason why we don't complete stuff or don't put it out there - ish can be uncomfortable. It **is** incomplete. It **is** imperfect. It will be flawed, particularly if someone with a judgmental and critical or assessing eye looks over the work done, they are absolutely certainly definitely going to find a fault or error in it and the least of which will be that it is not finished or not quite 'there' yet.

And that is ok. Really it is.

If you do like the perfectionism of a clean car and a tidy bench and a finished book on your night stand and arriving on time and looking neat and clean, then ish may dredge up some challenges and resistance in you. But even if you are a tad triggered by ish-ness you can be sure it will work for some -- or indeed many -- of the people you work with.

Ish is a lot of people out there. If it isn't you it most certainly is someone you know, or live with or work with or work alongside or travel with or share family names with or some other connection.

Yes, you most certainly know an ish kind of person.

Where 'not quite done' is just fine. Where unfinished is perfectly ok ... for now.

Ish is good enough... for now. It's underway.

So while I understand that ish is not the way some people like to do things, it is how some *other* people like to do things. It *is* how many people work. Any many of those people are in some seriously successful companies and organisations around the world.

It may not work every time, but it is a start. Ish is a beginning. It's a first draft, a version one, it's a rough concept or it's a prototype. It's an early iteration and a first pass. It's an initial draft and some first thoughts.

If you haven't already, allow some ish in.

I remember visiting my friend Alex, who needed to go to the supermarket. There we were in the car heading off to where I thought we'd been before -- the big name corporate giant supermarket. But no, this day we went a different way. We went down different streets and found ourselves in a different part of town.

And then we arrived at the supermarket. Yes, we had arrived at the supermarket that was part of a chain of called 'Not Quite Right'.

I shuddered. This was not a place I wanted to hang out or to be seen. How could you look at something or buy something and take it home and then use it if it wasn't 'quite right'? The horror!

But in we went. Alex picked up a shopping basket and he zoomed around that store like I'd never seen him move. He was on a mission. Looking for goods and products and tasty pantry treats. And all of them were not quite right. The tins were dented or the packages were torn or the dates for expiration were near or there were errors in the publishing on the packet or in the spelling of the product name.

In every case there was something not quite right with the goods he was shoving into that shopping basket. There were so many products in that basket he soon needed to upgrade to a shopping trolley so he had more space!

This was ish at it's best. The products he was buying were still ok; they were functioning, edible, passed the assessment of retailers and governing bodies, but they were a little quirky or incomplete or not quite there or not perfect – not quite right. Not quite.

I wondered as he continued to skid around the corners of each aisle with his trolley, 'yippeeeee'-ing as he skated on the linoleum squares, why was I not ok with this ish-ness?

Was it my perfect past? Had I always prided myself on buying branded goods and perfect quality and the best of the best and the most perfect and complete and precise?

Here it was in my face: Not Quite Right.

Was it a reflection on me? That I was willing to tolerate something imperfect? Did it mean *I* was imperfect or that I had low standards or didn't care?

What do you think of ish?

What does ish trigger in you?

Who wants to be wrong?

We learn in school that wrong is a punishable offence, it is an error and it reflects in your grades. You had to report in to your parents when you were wrong. In class you were scolded or belittled or teased in the breaks out in the yard. When you were wrong you were bad and broken and not quite right. How dreadful!

You were wrong. You were not the best. You were faulty or imperfect.

Alas, we were all wrong in our childhoods. And we were all right too.

We can be terribly hung up on being right. When I'm mentoring business owners, entrepreneurs and leaders, I'm so often working with comments and questions about 'is this right?' or 'I wanted to do it right', or 'It wasn't right so I changed it', or 'It was wrong.'

So many of us are obsessed with being right. Correct. Complete. Perfect. Done and in hand, finished and with no errors.

Oh the pressure! If we could move away from wrongs and rights; if we could extend our tolerance just a little more, our workplaces, families and the world would be so much easier to survive and thrive in. But our obsession with being right, perfect, correct - to avoid the humiliation or terror or teasing of being wrong, to be singled out, continues with us from the schoolyard well into adulthood.

There will be those who say you are or you aren't something. It happens with agile. You are agile or you aren't. And I'm saying I don't agree with that. Not the least of which is how binary and blocking it is. It says 'go away and come back when you are'. Or 'sit in the corner, you're wrong'. How un-collaborative, how unhelpful and lacking in hospitality that is!

Be a rebel and renegade

The world loves - and hates - a contrarian. But it is these people who lead and zig when the rest are zagging and forge the new that helps change the world. There is always someone or a group of someone's who starts the trend or who suggests the change. They may be a quiet voice early on, but before long there will be more voices. If Mother Theresa said 'Be the change you wish to see in the world' - and innumerable presenters will quote this in their inspiring presentations at all sorts of conferences - then you've got to do more being than just thinking or talking about change.

Yes you may need to be a bit of a renegade in this ishness.

If the most rule breaking we do is not following the verbal instructions the GPS or Google Maps is giving us, then we've got a way to go.

We are often brought up on following the rules, obeying the teacher, listening to our parents and doing what the boss says, that there isn't enough space or possibility to think that we could bend or break a rule or go against a trend.

Yet it is this exact style of rule-bending behaviour that has helped fuel the startup world. Businesses started by upstarts who bucked a trend or saw an opportunity or went with their gut or did the unthinkable.

Endless Instagram images tell us to be more gutsy, more against the grain and more of us, that I wonder who we are actually being if we're not being us.

Michael Port in his wonderful book *'The Contrarian Effect: Why It Pays (Big) to Take Typical Sales Advice and Do the Opposite'* applies to so many other elements of the world, not just sales.

And building a culture of agility and affecting any change in an organisation is a sales job!

Conventional advice is just that; conventional. Today's world needs more ingenious, creative and clever solutions, delivered quickly. And agility is just one of those. And it may be going against a deeply ingrained 'normal' in your organisation.

But hey ... you won't be *too* much of a rebel or renegade. Know there are thousands and thousands of people the world over thinking agile thoughts; there are people who've come before you and there will be people who will come after you. So while being agile can feel a tad rebellious or contrarian in your team or organisation, there's a global shift of agility underway and you best be on it!

It might not be perfect

Once bitten twice shy; there are many stories and war wounds from people who were part of an agile transformation and it didn't go well. So as a result they are over the whole approach and burned by the experience. The same occurs in so many aspects of life. You hear about a friend who went on a cruise and it didn't go well; puts you off cruises. Another friend didn't like the hotel at <insert your favourite city> and you swear you'll never go there.

My favourite restaurant and my husband Michael's too, is *Cafe Di Stasio* in Fitzroy Street, St Kilda, Melbourne, Australia. One look at my Instagram or Facebook feed would tell ya that. I like going there. The environment, the food, the people - we know them now after 10 - 15 years of going there regularly. The owner Ronnie Di Stasio is a maverick and leader in Italian culture, arts, ethics and hospitality. Many suggest we must have shares in the place but we simply love going there.

In fact, one time - in the 15 years I've been going there – just one time in 15 years, I didn't have a great experience. I felt ignored, hungry (perhaps I was hangry), ripped off. For a number of reasons the waiting service was poor, we didn't get to eat for quite a while and I started to get unhappy and then I felt pushed towards a particular menu choice without getting to see other menu options many other people were enjoying that day. The colleague I was with immediately slammed the restaurant and all it stood for. I knew better. This was one time for me that they weren't quite on their game. When I gave the feedback to the Maître-d and it found it's way to the owner, I received a phone call. And an apology next time. But it was in the apology that the insight came.

Just because you cook a bad meal once do you stop eating forever? No. You might make some adjustments to your own cooking. Same for the restaurant. Just because I'd had one less than enjoyable experience, I wasn't going to wipe them off totally. I've since returned again and again and just as always it hits the mark beautifully. Whereas my colleague declared she would never return... until the service improved.

But how will she know if the service has improved unless she goes back?

The same applies to agile.

You may criticize it and pay out and claim it's disastrous or didn't work or failed or was a stuff up; yet there are hundreds of thousands of people the world over applying the techniques, thinking and mindset and it's working for them. It may not be perfect.

In a first pass when you think and talk about agile, it IS a mindset.

So if your opening mindset is closed to agile, you're already not agile.

Keep an open mindset. Then you're more likely to be heading in the direction of agility.

Having a closed and set view or having a concrete opinion, or solid unchanging views and orthodox thoughts about exactly how it needs to be and you're not agile.

You can be a little more 'ish'

The people you work with need you to be a little more ish. The customers you serve want you to be and while your stakeholders or leaders might be fairly uncomfortable with the perceived risk with ish, it's a start. It's done and it's version one.

Once it's out there, we can get cracking on the next iteration. We can do version two. We can do something that is more-more, rather than more or less. We can add something more to it.

Ish is a start, a beginning and a commencement. You're in progress, you're on your way. Carry on.

There is a logic and common sense to ish.

It's a first draft. We create first drafts of things all the time: letters, emails, articles, wedding invitations, death notices, scripts, speeches, recipes, itineraries, instructions, plans, directions.

It means you've started and you're creating something and putting it out there.

Don't punish or reprimand or shame people for it not being fully operational and 100% correct.

Failure is sexy. The whole startup industry and the world of testing, experimenting and science know that failure leads to opportunity, to learning, to success. If we would only let it get started and let it be in progress, then we would have something to test, some results to look at.

Doing something is better than doing nothing.

40, 50, 80% done is better than even 20% done.

And 20% done is still better than nothing done at all.

Are you worrying what people think?

We're often advised by wise counsel to not worry what people with think. But we do. We do the opposite; we stress and work and tinker and do more and put more in and start again because it's not quite right and it gets us... where?

If we expect others to be perfect on their first attempt, that's unhelpful, unsupportive and lacking in encouragement. The best thing for someone with an idea is to start putting some of it into practice.

We're allowed to do that with our opinions. We put them out there while they're still forming or they're half-cooked.

By putting things out there in a state of ish, we'll learn more, test the market, be able to see if there's a true opportunity here and we'll be putting a minimum viable proposition (MVP) out there.

The Lean Startup movement popularized by Eric Ries in the book 'The Lean Startup' knows the power of the MVP. Get something out there and then you can test, iterate and get a more advanced version out there.

Build. Measure. Learn. It's a way of thinking and working that's a bit rough (likely) at the start, but it will improve and get better as the iterations go on.

This is ish.

It's in progress, it's underway, it's not fully cooked and it's open for improvement, change and review.

A youthful agility

I spent many a weekend as a child along the small side path of our weatherboard family home playing imaginary 'restaurants'. I had an old coffee percolator that I would fill with dirt in the top and then top up with tap water. I had old bowls from the kitchen, which I would add dirt and water to, and I had the plastic lids from square ice-cream containers.

The base, the square was the dog's water bowl and I got the lid. The lid was a plate. I would mix up that dirt from the garden with water from the tap and I'd make a mud pie. I'd mix and mix and then slap it out onto the square ice cream container lid.

Then I'd raid the garden, picking leaves and petals and flowers and I'd place them or push them down into the pat of mud to decorate the concoction, in an effort to make it look good enough to eat! Then I'd set them out in the sun to dry. Perhaps the next day I'd cut them up, serve them to my family and they'd make *'mmmm nom nom'* sounds as if they were eating my delicious mud pies. I was age 24.

No seriously, more likely six, seven or eight years old. Gee I loved doing that.

I was always making stuff -- from what I had available to me.

I'd often exclaim to my mother that *'I'm bored'!* To which she'd suggest a range of things I could do. I'd choose one of them and off I'd go, usually alone, making something up and bringing it to life.

Another thing I loved to do was create concerts. Our house had an elevated verandah at the front; five steps up and the verandah had a pergola over the top, letting in beautiful sunshine and light. At my feet was grass, that years later became concrete. But this verandah was the stage for so many improvised and made up concerts and performances. Singing, dancing, acting, morphing, making. It was all just play but it was making something out of nothing. Putting something 'out there'.

A childhood spent making and creating leads to an adulthood of the same. I just don't think you ever shake off the essence of those early interests, activities and drives.

They keep showing up in your adult life, like them or not, or whether you find a career that suits them or not.

While I didn't pursue professional acting or performing, I find it keeps showing up in the work I do with businesses and teams and projects. There is humour in learning and leadership; there are stories to tell in accents and there are games to be created and made and delivered in workshops and learning programs. Yes, I've found a great outlet for a lot of my creative juices from childhood.

So how do you go from enjoying making stuff, to setting up a business that works with businesses and teams? Why am I not an accountant or a police officer or an architect or chef? After all those mud pies, why didn't I pursue cooking?

I wasn't interested in that.

It was the making and creating, not the food.

It was the making and creating of the performance, not the actual theatre or the Broadway musical.

It was the making and the creating.

The taking of an idea and expressing it into the world. Whatever it is. However shite it was, it was done and it was out there.

So after a career working in communications, helping organisations get their messages out there - making and creating newsletters, publications, speeches, videos, events - I found that there was more to do than do it for people. Perhaps there was an opportunity to do it with people, or to help them do it better.

Over the past 10 years of my practice, speaking, facilitating and training on topics like collaboration, creativity, agile, communication, leadership ... at all times I'm driving through and helping people make and create; to help them get those ideas out of their heads and into reality. Whatever the ideas are. Let's get them into reality.

So agile-ish is a way to get your idea or possibility out into reality. And I know how to do that; I've been doing it all my life.

Hanging with geeks and improvisers

Disclosure - I'm a collaboration expert; I help people get sh*t done; I help them adapt and change and work together. As work changes, so must we. I like using creative tools. My bio says:

'*Lynne Cazaly is an international keynote speaker, author and facilitator. She is the author of the books:*

- *Agile-ish: How to create a culture of agility*
- *Leader as Facilitator: How to engage, inspire and get work done*
- *Making Sense: A Handbook for the Future of Work*
- *Create Change: How to apply innovation in an era of uncertainty, and*
- *Visual Mojo: How to capture thinking, convey information and collaborate using visuals.*

She works with executives, senior leaders and project teams on their major change and transformation projects. She helps people distil their thinking, apply ideas and innovation and boost the engagement levels and collaboration effectiveness of teams.

Lynne is an experienced board director and chair. She is a partner with Thought Leaders Global and on the Faculty of Thought Leaders Business School.'

I love helping people get through stuff and get from here to there. Often this is about a team or group or project that's trying to work together to get stuff done. It's not just any stuff but the good stuff, the stuff that will make a difference. So to facilitate teams and groups through making great progress, doing great work, that's rewarding. I love finding the barriers and obstacles and then identifying ways around them. There's a dodging and weaving, a nimbleness and agility in that too.

The reason I so love agile, agility and business agility is.... agilists get sh*t done.

I find red tape, bureaucracy, delaying tactics, excuses, blame, justifications, denial, distraction, procrastination and obfuscation some of the most irritating things. Grrrrr!

Ooooh don't get me started on a rant here, as I tap harder on the keys on my laptop writing this. The mere thought of having to talk to a customer service or automated system that just doesn't quite work or hasn't adapted to how customers like to access information drives me bananas.

The Australian Tax Office used to be like this. They are getting better. In the USA I think it's the motor branch; most countries will have a (usually) government department or service that seems to take forever to make things happen. They struggle to get sh*t done. Their teams aren't empowered; their leaders are indecisive. They're all constricted with red tape and silly, dated systems.

But hanging with software geeks who push out code and release the latest version of something everyday ... now that is super exciting. They get sh*t done. Constantly.

In the early 2000s I'd been an audience member in plenty of shows performed by the improvisation troupe, *Impro Melbourne*. They mentioned at the end of a performance how their next term of courses and workshops were starting; you mean you can learn this stuff? How? If it's improvised, how the heck do you learn it?

After a year of workshops and courses, I knew how. They follow a set of principles, philosophies that mean they can step on stages with complete strangers and a single line of dialogue or a prop and pull off a deeply touching, creative and extensive (two minutes to half an hour) scene that takes you through a rollercoaster of emotions.

Here I was finding some sweet intersections between what agilists do and what improvisers do.

Both believe in having the right kind of mindset to begin with, and then they set about putting their thinking out there into the world, strung up between a raft of general-sounding principles and ideologies.

What seemed like magic was now being unpicked and unpacked. And I loved it even more!

Improvisers get sh*t done, delivering value for their audiences, working together.

Agilists get sh*t done, delivering value for their customers, working together.

How good is this!

Now, let's find out how and we can apply that to many other types of business that are tying themselves up in red tape. Let's break free of that stuff so we can be w-a-y more agile-ish.

There's an irony here though among all this adaptability and agility I'm speaking of.

Most experts, consultants, authors and speakers would have an irony. Whatever it is you're banging on about, you might find you suck at it.

The window washer's windows are dirty; the mechanic's car breaks down; the collaboration expert likes to work alone; the adventurer has a fear of heights; the surgeon doesn't like going to the doctor; the chef hates cooking at home; the accountant's books are in a sorry state; the productivity expert is wasting time on stuff that doesn't matter.

(Not referring to anyone I know in any of these; seriously. Irony is a thing and you need to be aware of it; I sure am).

What's that saying about teachers? Those who don't do, teach.

The suggestion that even if you can't or won't or don't do the 'thing', you can sure as eggs teach someone else how to do it.

So here's an irony with agility and me writing this book.

I don't like change with the best of them.

But if I am to survive and thrive in my business I must change and adapt to the pressures in the market.

It's so easy to fall into a habit and stay there.

Or eat the same thing from your local takeaway.

Or drive the same way to work.

Or say the same types of things in your workshops or presentations.

Or think the same way every freakin' day of your life.

So how do we do agile and agility with this challenging irony that we will all have... to some degree?

I am challenged by the new, unless it's on a topic I like. I too don't like trying some types of foods, travelling to some parts of the world or doing some things that challenge or confront me. But it is in this exact space that agility lives. It's called uncertainty! And adopting an agile mindset and agile way of working or being is the best way to respond in uncertainty.

CHANGE

Whole world problems

There are so many reasons why agile and agility is on so many agendas, strategies, bullet journals and 'to do' lists.

Productivity - getting stuff done

There is a busy-ness attitude sweeping the world and while it might be a foolish badge of honor to wear, being busy has been on trend. If you've got lots on, you must be great, clever, in demand. Yet so much of our busy-ness is wasteful. Rushing, juggling, multi-tasking and doing things for others first rather than ourselves.

Accompanying busyness is the rise in the productivity movement. There are workshops and sessions on how to empty your email inbox, how to hack yourself and the system and how to complete your workout in one tenth of the time; six minutes that is.

But in this rush to do lots of 'stuff', how much of it is actually 'good stuff'?

The 'Get Shit Done' meme needs an edit and change to 'Get *Good* Shit Done'.

Just do the good stuff; the stuff that will deliver the greatest value, the greatest results, impact, lasting change or outcomes. If not, then don't do it. Or at least put it way down on your 'To Do' list or even on your 'Don't' list so it doesn't distract you from the good stuff.

Delivery and Velocity - meeting their needs, now

Joining the busy culture is the culture of now. *'I want it now'.* We get fed up waiting just a few seconds for a web page to load or an elevator to arrive and don't even get me started about road works, diversions, traffic lights and speed limits. Get me where I want to be, when I want to be there... or quicker if you can, please.

While a chef and the team in a kitchen might be slaving away putting a brilliant meal together, we're sitting there wanting it now. We want cars on demand, couriers to arrive, food delivered to our door, music to listen to now and movies and other forms of entertainment to watch and play, now. Quicker than now actually; we want it ready when we're ready.

Quality - do it well

And we want it all to work. Really well. I'm busy, I want it now and it had better be good. The booking system needs to work, the website needs to be easy and function well and the technology needs to be near faultless.

Priority – are we working on the right things?

As a result of demanding customers, consumers, communities and countries, we need to ask in our organisations... 'are we actually working on the right things?'

'And how do we know they're the right things?'

Perhaps we're distracted... with that thing over there... working on some other stuff that doesn't provide great value to customers or the market. Perhaps we've been busy for months, doing what we thought was great work, but how valuable is it really?

Caught up in red tape

Perhaps we're trying to do the right stuff but the systems around us tie us up in knots, drag us over speed humps and send us on diversions and detours that slow us down, kill our creativity and batter our soul. Who has the energy to keep fighting annoying processes and systems that don't support innovation and progression or encourage responsiveness and adaptability?

In the Harvard Business Review article *'Do You Know How Bureaucratic Your Organization Is?'* by Gary Hamel and Michele Zanini, it's startling to read about the cost of red tape and cumbersome systems. While the incentives for dismantling bureaucracy are high, the challenges are high too. They say:

> *'Upending cultural norms isn't easy. It takes courage, a dose of righteous indignation, and, perhaps most critical, data. People pay attention to things that can be measured. To dismantle bureaucracy, then, the first step is to be honest about how much it's costing your organization.*
>
> *These costs fall into seven categories:*
>
> 1. *Bloat: too many managers, administrators, and management layers*
> 2. *Friction: too much busywork that slows down decision making*
> 3. *Insularity: too much time spent on internal issues*
> 4. *Disempowerment: too many constraints on autonomy*
> 5. *Risk Aversion: too many barriers to risk taking*
> 6. *Inertia: too many impediments to proactive change*
> 7. *Politics: too much energy devoted to gaining power and influence.'*

While some in your organisation will be keen to stick with 'the way things are' because change sucks and is hard, others will be delightfully surprised at the horrid costs once these are measured and presented.

In workshops and planning sessions, I love taking a team of senior leaders through these seven costs and see which of them they're willing to make changes on, now, today. They quickly identify plenty of situations where these costs are tripping up their teams from making great progress. It's even better when those leaders can gain feedback from their teams about the things that are slowing them down or getting in their way.

Working on too many things - no priority

Perhaps we're working on too many things. Beware the scattered team or diluted organisation. Lots of people, all working on stuff. And how long have you been working on it? What's the sunk cost, the ego attached to it? Is it going to look bad to stop going down this path to turn around and come back and then head off in another direction?

Don't underestimate the loss of face, the pride, ego and status that is at risk when the 'we were wrong' or the 'it's not working as we'd hoped' type of decisions need to be made and messages need to be communicated.

These types of issues indicate a culture that's not agile ... enough. The psychological safety of saying 'it didn't work' isn't available.

It's truly time to get more agile-ish. Add some more of the agile mindset, philosophies, ways of thinking, being and doing that will drive your organisation towards greater value and a more successful business delivering great value for your clients and customers.

Change is stealth-like

Customers increasingly want you to respond, now. Yesterday.

Business has to respond quicker, with things that the customer hasn't even thought they needed. Simply relieve their pain, frustration, and irritation – and do it quicker.

I can't seem to live without Apple Pay on my phone now, tapping away buying stuff without needing to take my wallet. Too easy.

In the 1990's I was lecturing in advertising and communication at Holmesglen Technical and Further Education (TAFE) College in Australia. The set reading for students in my class was Bill Gates' book 'The Road Ahead'.

Oh my freakin' wow! How I loved that book and all it predicted and suggested about where technology was going and how we were going to get there.

How did he know what was possible? His description in particular of the 'pocket wallet' was captivating. We wouldn't need cash or card and this was so dreamy to me. To think I could get on a plane without a paper boarding pass. Impossible? Aaaah not impossible. That's how we board now.

Yes we see people with folders of paper and their travel itineraries but I'm happy to app and tap and get on board stat.

What seemed crazy or impossible or futuristic then is arriving quicker than we thought it would. It's at the point now where things are already here; they are arriving before we thought they'd be possible, let alone in production or in prototype or being used and trialed and adopted. And with those changes in technology or products come new businesses, startups and smart players bold enough to take action.

New entrants to the market are arriving constantly. There are plenty of start-ups that have already started that you're not aware of. They're hunting out investors and funders and they're lining up their ducks to announce and go to market.

The work that's going on behind the scenes is lethal. You've got no idea what they're doing. It's only when they go public or their founder blogs on Medium or tweets their boarding passes for an upgrade or because they've finally scored an entree to a business class lounge that you could get a hunch that they're on the way up. Seriously up. But you'd have to be following a few thousand of them. And who's got time to be checking all of the yet - to - rise stars of startups.

I followed with interest the wonderful steady rise of Flamingo, Dr Catriona Wallace after meeting her at a Commonwealth Bank Women in Focus conference (180 awesome women who are movers and shakers). Via her social media posts I could see the hard yards and Pacific miles she clocked up back and forth between Australia and the west coast of the USA. Hard work. Quiet work.

Not much about her startup seemed public until the launch and announcement. And there she was on the front cover of a magazine or six and her wonderful story about building and transforming a small fintech startup into a listed customer experience company on the Australian Stock Exchange – capitalized at over $24million.

Sure, you could be hanging around business incubators and accelerators or hubs and co-working spaces to see if you can pick up where the next big thing is going to come from but even that is a waste of your precious time.

If you're trying to head someone off at the pass or avoid being surprised, you'll be disappointed.

Businesses, apps, individuals, solutions, software, features, programs, products and other problem solving wonders are hitting the marketplace every moment of every day. The days of product launches where a business posted a media release online are gone. You'd be better to keep your eyes on the rising stars and listicles in magazines that list the best of the newcomers to even get a hint about what they're up to.

Yes there are plenty of people in garages all over the world, in spare rooms, in co-working spaces and in cafes creating stuff using remote and distributed workforces. They don't need an office building, they don't need to rent anything; they don't need a fancy car or even anything more than a device or a laptop. They're managing a team of people working on their idea and paying the Upwork or Fiverr rates and a virtual assistant rather than having a cast of plenty working in some secret warehouse location. It's happening right in front of you. Right next door to you. So your ability to respond by the time you hear about it is pretty much lost.

There is a nondescript shop in Albert Park Village, a shopping strip near where I live. There are people inside the shop front working at desks; there's a couch in the front window and there's no signage or branding on the shop to say what it is. Last year they asked a question via a small sign in the window: *'What do you think we do in here?'*

Locals passing by had contributed their thoughts via some Post-it notes and those Post-its slowly started crowding out the initial sign. There were suggestions of 'studying', 'religious group', 'hanging out', 'doing drugs', 'learning', 'fixing computers', 'creating apps', 'designing websites'... and on the answers went.

In a way people were right and wrong.

The small shop is a co-working space of startups. They're all launching something. They're all creating, initiating, starting and growing something and that is so freakin' exciting!

New market entrants are continuing to look a lot different to the ones you may have read about in MBA textbooks with Michael Porter's name on the front cover!

The days of responding to market entrants of the last century are done. You've got to forge your own path of innovation and be adaptive and respond to the various impacts and changes rather than a specific market threat.

As you respond to the market's needs - not the new market entrants - you need to engage more deeply with customers. This doesn't mean asking them what they want you to make. Rather, hang out with them... watch them, listen to them and pay attention to the areas where there is friction or where things are difficult for them. That's where the opportunities lie. That's how to be more responsive and adaptive.

Care factor: a lot

There can be a sense of 'why should I care: I've got a job and a mortgage and my paycheck. Who cares if my employer is agile or not?'

But any business that survives is adapting, constantly.

Change is hard. Yes, it's really hard.

In the Harvard Business Review article *'Changing Company Culture Requires a Movement, Not a Mandate'* by Bryan Walker and Sarah A Soule, they state:

'For organizations seeking to become more adaptive and innovative, culture change is often the most challenging part of the transformation. Innovation demands new behaviors from leaders and employees that are often antithetical to corporate cultures, which are historically focused on operational excellence and efficiency.'

So yes there is a 'foot on the gas/foot on the brake' thing going on.

The road is littered with all of those Fortune 500 companies who are sliding down the list. There is also an ocean of smaller and medium sized businesses who - despite any agility, or being highly agile - just didn't find their place or space in the market. Businesses, ideas, initiatives fail all the time. But it's the adaptation, the changeability that makes them more hardy to survive the next wave of change.

Drones and details

Back in June 2017 I saw a news item on evening television about needing regulations for drones because crazy people are flying them into buildings, across airfields and into no-fly zones. Hello? Drones have been commercially available for.... ummmm years.

Even a year ago at an entrepreneurial conference we learned about getting a drone license and some of the general etiquette to it.

More than three years ago I was drone buzzed at the local beach by an eager pilot who was still learning the intricacies of flying the thing.

And similarly, about three years ago, some of the fellow travellers on one of our many outback trips across the Australian deserts brought along a drone and launched it. They took some brilliant footage with it.

So yes, they've been around a while.

But regulators are just realising now that they need to have rules and guidelines in place. I understand many governments will have been talking about it for a lot longer, but this is the perfect example of an opportunity for agility.

There's none or little significant action taken.

They simply talk about it some more saying 'something needs to be done'. That's a little too inactive for me.

Whatever the debate that rages about drones and where they can fly and who can do what, they serve as just one of so many examples; change is coming, change happens and we are too often too slow to respond and adapt.

And that's for introducing new regulations, training our teams to be able to handle the challenges of the future or listening to our customers to better understand their challenges.

The end of the news item about 'something needs to be done' regarding drones, featured a professional drone pilot, fully credentialed and regulated saying that perhaps the 'horse had bolted'. It will be interesting to see how regulators play catch up.

It's an example of where adaptability is needed... sooner.

Don't be intimidated
by what you don't know.
That can be your
greatest strength
and ensure that you
do things differently
from everyone else.

- Sara Blakely, Spanx

It's a change thing...

Change and transformation is a constant in organisations, and the reality is that leaders need to lead it. And get used to leading it.

While the team might enact the change, it's the leader who needs to engage and execute on the change. And it's through change that organizational culture is created.

Your capability as a leader is often measured by how well you lead change and transformation, and how well you've helped a team or organization shift from here... to there.

Over time, it can be challenging to keep on leading change and transformation projects - particularly if the team is feeling a little change weary!

Some team members resist and pushback on the change initiatives you're leading. This type of resistance and response can build and next thing you know, you have a groundswell of support against a change, not for it.

Leading change is a daily part of being a contemporary leader. And leaders need to feel comfortable with the discomfort that can come from their efforts of leading change. Even when the going is tough.

We're living in a VUCA world (volatility, uncertainty, complexity and ambiguity) and to lead change in this environment takes a mix of mindset, know-how and action that positions leaders as the true transformers of organizational culture.

If you don't like change, you are going to like irrelevant even less.

- Eric Shinseki

Old change don't work

Once upon a time there was a big business of a few thousand staff and a few hundred million dollars in turnover. They wanted to be agile. They currently weren't. I spoke with them about helping them with this 'journey' they knew they needed to embark on.

They requested a plan - of what would happen when and how it would happen, who would be involved and how much it would cost.

What is wrong with this story?

The way you lead change says everything about your culture. Change brings renewal; if you want to change culture, change how you lead change.

— Lynne Cazaly

What's wrong with this story is they wanted to be agile and wanted to do that in a very controlled and predictable way and know about it all in advance.

Almost immediately we needed to talk about how leading this change program would give them the opportunity to experience a new culture, a new way of working, and feel what it's like to be agile. Ish.

As it turned out, I didn't proceed to work with this organisation. It wasn't a 'fit' or a 'match' or some other gentle way of saying 'no thank you'. They're not at fault, but they're not ready.

A few months later, a couple of the team who were aiming to drive this change left the organisation. As they said, 'they're not even ready for us yet'.

The leaders in the organisation were not ready for this. They're not ready for the transformation they need to make.

Now it's one, two years later and I suspect a pocket of the business will be ready. In the meantime, they've had further staff changes, felt more competitive pressure and have spent some time clearly getting closer to their customers. I'm also one of their customers. And they're trying to get closer. This is great news.

Lead change to transform culture

Leaders lead change.

Leaders influence culture.

And culture can be transformed through change.

When leaders lead change, they can change culture. They demonstrate that they are open to change, welcoming of possibility, curious to what might be.

Productivity can be high. Changes stick and the transformation program delivers. Teams find that they have traction and then massive forward progress is made.

So rather than allowing change to be a burden or challenge, change can be the catalyst to shifting culture.

I say, to change culture, change how you lead change.

As a leader, you need more than just a model of change that shows what happens to people during change; you need a practical model of change that will guide you, inspire you and help you design, communicate and facilitate the change. This includes more creative, responsive, adaptive and agile methods and tools for a dynamic and changing workplace.

The challenges of change

How do you help people understand why this change is just as, or more important than the last one you led? There's only so much 'urgency' you can create as a reason to change, or to push or engage people to change.

And sometimes it's a challenge to get strong buy-in from across the whole team. There might be pockets of support, pockets of dissent and a bunch of people just sitting in the middle, waiting to see which side of the change fence they might sit on.

Sustaining high levels of engagement throughout a change program is a challenge. Questions can come from all quarters. You might want to answer every question that people have but sometimes that's not possible. It may feel like you have little time or you may feel there's a sense that the questions would never end, and that you would get the same questions over and over and over....

How do you handle the resistance, the comments, questions and frustrations of team members... without letting it get on top of you, disrupting the rest of the team, or putting a stop to the transformation that's underway?

Leading change isn't something that's often taught – there's plenty about leadership and management and time management and performance management. But where you do you learn the critical elements to lead change?

Much is learned from the leaders who lead us. And much of that can be flawed ...there's only so much that a PowerPoint slide with the Elizabeth Kubler-Ross model of grief can do to help you lead change! As highly regarded as the model is, it's about death and dying. Enough with linking change to death. How uninspiring!

We've got to move on from the 'death' model of change to a more contemporary approach, of change being constant, living, dynamic and a necessity.

Change and transformation needs to be led ... every day. And leaders need to do that in an inspiring way.

There is a real risk or fear that the change program you're leading could fail. Some of them do. And if you're judged on performance or capability to lead a team through a rapidly changing environment, this can impact credibility, marketability, success and career path.

Leaders need to design, engage and execute change in a human, authentic way, yet still maintain a strong sphere of leadership influence among peers and beyond. It's a fine balance between leading the team, leading the change and leading your own career.

Transformation tipping points

The path or ladder to true transformation can be treacherous... and time wasting. I think it can look a lot like a ladder where you can be wallowing on the ground or stuck on a particular rung.

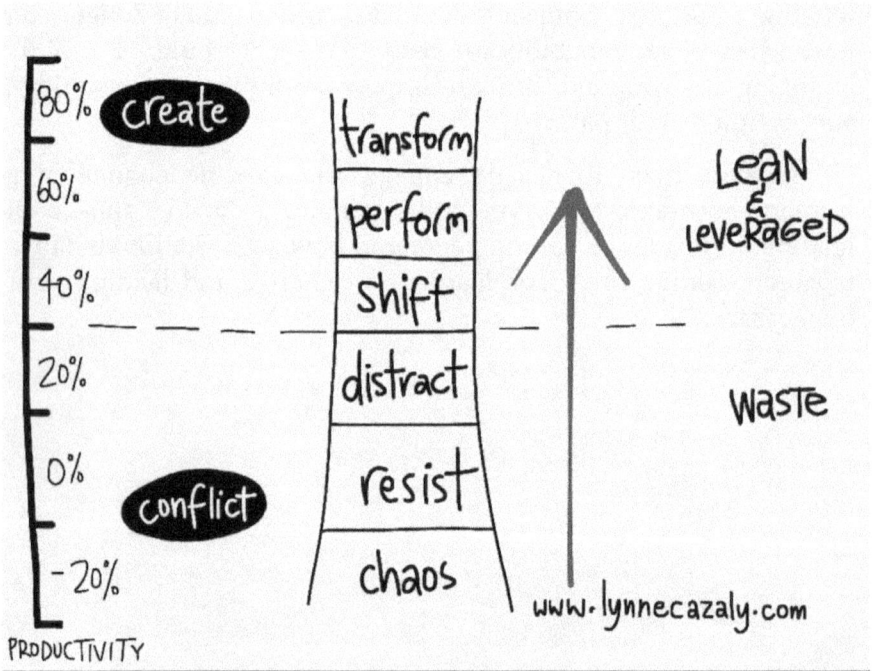

At the bottom of the ladder are organizations and teams in **chaos**; they're losing ground and on the decline. They are resistant to change, fearful and frightened of change and don't know where to begin. They're moving in reverse. These are the businesses that go 'belly up', that become insolvent and are wound up. Too soon they're gone.

There are plenty of businesses close to chaos but they're attempting change and transformation. They're stuck. When teams and organizations **resist** change – which often happens in the early stages of a change or transformation - there is a sense of being in neutral; poor levels of productivity and a feeling of not getting anywhere. Going in circles, simple changes not being adopted and it's all too easy to continue the old ways of working. Why change?

Progressing up the ladder or path of change are organizations and teams that are intent on change and transformation but they're... **distracted**. They're too busy looking at competitors and not responding, or they're focused on internal changes that deliver little impact (or are unnecessary in the first place), or their attention is taken off the positive process of change by other troubles: industrial, legal, financial or media crises. They're busy all right, but productivity suffers because they're focusing on distracting things.

If you think of an organization as aiming to make forward progress through change and transformation, each of these stages of the change path or ladder see the business slipping, with wheels spinning; engine revving loudly – just not getting anywhere!

And that's where we get to a tipping point.

Up over this point in change and transformation is where productivity changes, focus is shifted and positive friction is achieved, traction is gained.

At the **shift** stage, organizations and teams are making changes and transformation. They're bringing new processes and ways of working to the business ... but it's still a hard slog. Change is not the norm; the dynamic of progressive change isn't being leveraged and change takes significant effort to get traction and to stick.

Once the team gets to **perform**, productivity goes up, change initiatives begin to 'stick' in a positive way and the path to being able to transform culture is paved. Positive change initiatives build on previous changes made and the culture is a high performing one. There is acceptance of change as the norm; 'this is what we do. We change. We keep changing because that's how we do things around here.'

Ultimately, organizations and teams that reach **transform** do so because they are agile and adaptive; they make change stick, and then reinvent, experiment and review to make change an ongoing part of how they work.

Some people will have to go

Yes some people won't have the mindset for this agile-ish thing. They won't have the attitude, the capability, and the wherewithal. Yes, skills are learnable, but if you've worked with someone who you thought just didn't 'get it' you might be getting close to what could happen with a change and transformation towards agility

Some people will have to go.

And this hurts many managers and leaders and of course the people who have to go. The least of which hurts because they know they'll have to have a difficult conversation, but more so because if you have an agile mindset you'll already know that it will be hard for people - who you don't think will fit – to respond well to being moved on from the new world of agile-ish. They aren't agile in mindset and so leaving the organisation they'll need to find somewhere else, and that in itself is an agile act, an agile way of being. How you respond to adversity and change says so much about your mindset.

As a result, take good care. Take good care of people. Do what you can to help them find their way, find their next thing or find something else.

Have empathy and care about this.

It's not just numbers and resources and stock and head count. These are people are some of them will have to go because they will not support the agile journey.

You may not know who they are right now, but they will present themselves as you go through the journey to agile. And then you'll know. And you'll have to do something about it. You'll have to respond and adapt.

Stay relevant

Endless articles and listicles on Artificial Intelligence and Machine Learning paint a worrying state for those who don't change. Unfortunately though, they may not be aware of changes underway because they're blinded or resistant to change. But wherever you are, whatever industry you're in, change is underway. Transformation is happening and we have to adapt to stay relevant.

If we want a career with purpose, a life of purpose, we'll need to do some sort of work or service and it's smart to stay abreast of the changes and transformation occurring in your industry and field.

There's something about comfort zones in this too.

Watching *Ninja Warrior* on Australian television recently the often quoted statement of *'get out of your comfort zone; that's where you grow'* was shouted by an enthusiastic, leopard-print wearing, pony-tailed fit as anything young woman. Yeeeeha! She was up for the challenge.

The course scared the living daylights out of her but she committed to the preparation and lead up; the endless fitness sessions and strength sessions to help her build her dexterity and strength so she could find her way across the challenging fitness obstacles in record time. Then on the big night of the event, she crashed out on the second obstacle. Awwww! Oooooh! Nooooo! How do you think all that wonderful preparation changed her?

Regardless of the outcome, she'd been pushing herself out of her comfort zone for months. If she'd just showed up to the event and gone *'oh yeah I'll have a go'*, she'd have missed all the times she crushed her comfort zone. She's already a different person, so learning new things, working in different ways and thinking differently are a part of us all stepping beyond where we are now. We're changing anyway; our cells and skin and brain are constantly changing; why not also change the way we think and make our future a little more adaptive, responsive, agile?

Yes change is hard. In 'Immunity to Change' by Lisa Laskow Lahey and Robert Kegan - the groundbreaking and oft-quoted text in HR teams the world over - they confirm for us that change is tricky.

'Development does not unfold continuously; there are periods of stability and periods of change. When a new plateau is reached we tend to stay on that level for a considerable period of time.

However, many, if not most, of the change challenges you face today and will face tomorrow require something more than incorporating new technical skills into your current mindset. These are the "adaptive challenges," and they can only be met by transforming your mindset, by advancing to a more sophisticated stage of mental development.

So it is not change by itself that makes us uncomfortable; it is not even change that involves taking on something very difficult. Rather, it is change that leaves us feeling defenseless before the dangers we "know" to be present that causes us anxiety.

Here we are reminded of what the psychologist William Perry once said are the two most important things to know about people you are trying to help change: "What do they really want, and what will they do to keep from getting it?'

Move faster

The clichés around disruption have been building over this decade - you need to disrupt or you will be disrupted.

Dan Lyons, author of *'Disrupted: My Misadventures in the Start-Up Bubble'* wrote a column in Fortune Magazine titled *'How to Master Change'*. Among other things, Lyons says that so many businesses are talking about transformation because for a lot of them it's a matter of life and death. *'Their legacy business is fading, and they need to become something new.'*

For that reason alone, you'd want to find out how best to remain adaptive, responsive and swift-moving so you can pounce on and grab opportunities -- or at least sniff out the first whiff of an opportunity.

Lyons cites how certain companies are great at transformation and likens them to the actual toys from Hasbro that begin as a robot and then get bent into the shape of a car. Transforming indeed! By name and nature.

But best is the example of Santa Clara, Californian chip company Nvidia. Although it's 23 years old, its humble history from making graphics boards for video game fans was just the background it needed. They evolved in 2006 by hooking their chips together and making a supercomputer. Still later, another ten years later, the business is still going strong. Their graphics processors power so many computers on this planet.

So how do *they* continue to evolve and remain agile? Ish?

They've kept their ears to the ground, their eyes open and their noses tuned in to the whiff of opportunity. And there it is; in the shape of an autonomous vehicle. To make an automated car work, manufacturers know the vehicle needs to gather a h-u-g-e amount of data from all of the sensors and cameras on the vehicle. That's how these vehicles 'see' stuff. Nvidia's graphics chips are ideal for this type of work. Eighty different companies - including the likes of Tesla and Audi are using the Nvidia technology.

Nvidia's success comes down to these things:

Big ears

Not just listening widely to the world, but tuning in deeply to customers. Thanks to the ongoing relationships they've had with automotive companies, they've been able to keep tabs on what the industry needed.

Impatient boss

I love this characteristic! The CEO, Jen-Hsun Huang still runs the business like a start-up. While he founded it all those 23 years ago, he's still running it in a nimble, agile and adaptive way.

Active imaginations

To be a great transformer, to remain agile you've got to find other uses for the capabilities you already have. This is adapting to the circumstances and to the changing and volatile environment. Nvidia have done just that. Transform like crazy!

As Lyons wraps up the article he says, I

That's a nice little story about agility, but keep your eye on them; they may or may not keep changing. Who knows where they'll be in a year or three or eight?

Many a conference speaker has quoted Kodak compared to Instagram and how Airbnb owns no property and Uber owns no cars. These are some of the classic examples quoted for why businesses need to keep adapting.

Whatever example you want to use, if you're spending too much time trying to find more examples of why you should be agile, someone else in the same building or same city or same field - or adjacent industry - is being more agile than you are while you hunt for more evidence.

Get on with it. You'll need to move faster to deal with disruption.

Not quite fast enough

Someone who didn't think they moved fast enough is Starwood former CEO, Frits Van Paasschen. Authoring a book on how businesses can thrive, even in times of disruption, he picked up on a time when perhaps he hadn't moved quite fast enough.

'The Disruptors' Feast: How to Avoid Being Devoured in Today's Rapidly Changing Global Economy', tells his story from the perspective of seeing changes approaching saying something about it. Perhaps it was a lessons learned or a cathartic experience.

Yet must have been foundation shaking. Starwood Hotels... you might be wondering 'huh, who are they'. Well they were gobbled up by competitor Marriott International and as all hotels are, being disrupted by Airbnb (which happens to have the same market valuation of the *combined* Starwood and Marriott at January 2017). *Gulp

It's not all about hotels from him though as he worked in brewing and at Nike, Disney, McKinsey and so there are plenty of stories to share.

I'd think that most senior leaders would have war stories to share over the next few years. As disruptions are dealt and upper hands are taken by competitors and new players, many a company leader, CEO or exec is going to have 'lessons learned' to share. They just don't know it yet. In fact, they're likely in the middle of learning about them. Right now. This is what sense making is about - you don't know what's happening until you can get some space, and get some hindsight. This is clearly what Van Paasschen has got.

Here's what he said he didn't quite notice quickly enough:

'I didn't see the power of digital technology and change as clearly coming out of the [2008 financial] crisis as I wish I had. If you could rerun the past and create less dependence, from a hotel company

71

perspective on the OTAs [online travel agencies], that would obviously be something that I would have loved to be able to do. I think seeing the rise of Airbnb before it became the extraordinary force of change that it is obviously would have served me well, or all of us well for that matter, too.'

He suggests that the book is a *'wake-up call for people to recognize that the things that keep us from responding to disruption are pervasive in how we view the world.'*

Yes, let's stay awake lest our industry be devoured by a pesky, global start up.

Changing in uncertainty

Leaders leading in uncertain times and unknown situations are needing more flexible capabilities; a mindset of being able to flex and shift no matter what's happening.

To lead into the unknown - whatever your industry, field, expertise or role - here are five capabilities for keeping it together when you're not sure what's up ahead:

1. Start Before You're Ready

You can't wait for the script to arrive. You've got to get momentum and get doing.

Ray Bradbury, the science fiction, horror and fantasy writer, said, 'First you jump off the cliff and you build your wings on the way down'. And although some believe the quote attributable to Kurt Vonnegut, another equally interesting and creative author, the message is the same: leap and the net will appear, you will adapt, you'll work it out and you'll be moving. We are adaptable humans. Our survival depends on it.

2. Like Surprises

Scriptwriters call them 'plot twists' and we notice them as shocks, surprises or bolts from the blue. Once you've started before you're ready and you're in motion, some unexpected stuff will happen along the way. How spontaneous are you? Do you insist on sticking with the plan or are you open to other ways, paths and possibilities?

3. Try Something Else

Experimenting helps you refine, edit and alter your thinking, offers, service, design or idea. It's rare for the first version to be the final version... of anything. In a world that's slowly becoming more accepting of failure as a learning process, you've got to see what works as well as what doesn't. As Keith Johnstone, teacher and godfather guru of improvisation says *'Do something, rather than having lengthy discussions about doing something'.*

4. Go Co

'If you want to see the future coming, 90% of what you need to learn you'll learn from outside your industry', says Gary Hammel, author of *'Leading the Revolution'.*

Working with diversity invites varied views, talents, experiences, cultures and backgrounds to the table or conversation to co-create good work. 'Co' is all about together. Working with others is a... co-brainer. It's impossible for us to do it all by ourselves. Plus, others need your expertise to make what they're doing brilliant too!

5. Be Curious

Acting like a risk taker and brave explorer in times of uncertainty can feel like it's too big a risk to take; but bold actions can also reap huge rewards. Leaders who set up an environment where others can succeed are staying open to what that team can do. That means stepping into some uncertainty, some unknown and some unsure.

There's nothing to fear when you're leading into the unknown.

The opposite of fear isn't bravery; it's curiosity.

In value we stifle

Though we try to encourage our team and say we welcome and promote curiosity and failure and creativity, when it comes down to it, I think we can tend to stifle, strangle and stop it. It can seem so risky, particularly when we are being (financially) rewarded for success or for hitting certain targets. If we certainly hit the target, we certainly get the reward. If we dabble in uncertainty and failure and experiments and 'who knows what will happen' type of activities, then we face uncertainty in recognition and rewards, and in our personal branding and career progression... and our pocket.

One of my earliest leaders in local government had clearly read some of the great 1970s mantras in being a leader or manager. She would say 'my door is always open' and 'we value honesty around here' and 'I'm dressed in work clothes today because we might need to jump in and get our hands dirty'.

These were all platitudes, clichés and unfounded and unsupported statements. She'd say it but never live it.

Her door wasn't always open - literally or figuratively. Some days it was closed so she could do quiet work; and that's ok, that's not what the issue is here. It was what was said and what was welcomed or invited that were at odds.

You couldn't raise topics with her without her going wild with anger or criticism; you couldn't be honest about stuff without her immediately laying blame in your direction or pointing fingers at your own behaviours; and she may have been dressed in work clothes but always sat behind her desk pointing at the team to go and do the things that we hoped she might step in and do or demonstrate occasionally.

Despite this story from one of my first bosses being from last century, it's how many leaders are leading today... in this century.

We think we have these open minds, ideas and beliefs and that what we are doing is creating value for the people and projects around us, but are we really?

You can see this in workplaces every day in meetings. The leader of the meeting will declare it's about innovation or new ideas or creativity or 'we want to hear everyone's voices' or 'different views are welcomed'. But when the meeting is underway and the realities and bad habits are in full swing... it doesn't seem to go that way.

In an attempt to generate value, we often stifle it.

Tinkering or transforming?

The need for change in organisations and sectors all over the world has created a whole field of expertise and a category of employee - The Change Manager, the Change Leader, the Change Consultant. They live and breathe this stuff; they know what it's about, how to do it and the impact a change initiative can have on people and the way organisations operate. They're all about helping us get from here ... to there.

Some change leaders don't just deal with change anymore, they deal with even bigger stuff ... **transformation.**

Yes, change has grown bigger and become even more chang-ey; change that is more significant and more widespread and interconnected and ongoing is transformation.

(Possible cliché alert regarding 'transformation': please don't use a picture of a caterpillar and a butterfly to show how you are transforming a project, system or people. Yikes. Cliché alert. Whoop! Whoop!)

Change: to make or become different.

In one of my earlier careers as an awards judge for communication projects, the panel would review submissions where entrants would declare that their goals were to 'change the community's perception of....' or 'change the customer's behaviour' or 'change the way that...'- yet few of these declarations of change seemed to also declare by what amount or percent or scale they would change, to make or become different.

It seemed that a little bit of change was still change and for many in the field, that was enough. Tick. Done. Change has occurred. Next project!

Change often seems to have a defined and finite scope.

But to transform is something else. It's often seen as something different.

Transformation means 'marked change'.

Is transformation a change you can see? Is it obvious, noticeable, significant, ongoing and interconnected? Could you perhaps keep track of it or mark it on something: *'A year ago we were there, last month we were there and now ...we are here! Look! Transformation.'*

Do you remember the pencil marks on the kitchen wall? As you grew in height you could see that transformation had occurred, and a marked change had taken place. You might have done this for your own kids, or pets or plants or even your unread book collection.

Transformation is change. But I fear that while we're all so involved and committed to a piece of change, it's actually just ... a tinkering.

Tinker. Tinker. Tinker.

A tinkerer was somewhat of a gypsy; they'd travel from place to place and make a living by fixing and mending metal pots and pans and tools. The noise was a 'tinker'.

You can hear it - when someone is working on an old car under the hood, or they are rattling around in the utensils drawer in the kitchen looking for a potato masher or a pot lid or the spoon that completes that set of salad servers. Rattle rattle clank clang and tinker. Yes that noise.

Tinkering was about improving, to try to mend, to fix it up or improve. A little.

Of all the effort that goes into change and transformation programs in workplaces, this is what I see: lots of effort. To improve. Hours and days, weeks and months of time and effort. So many meetings, information packs, version control of the information packs, flow charts and arrows, more meetings, working groups, town halls and whole-of-staff gatherings, more meetings and presentations and packs.

But not enough of decisions, actions, experiments and results. As a recent *Harvard Business Review* suggests, many of our changes aren't ambitious enough.

Many changes or shifts are too delicate, bite size - just a morsel or a crumb. The end result: tinkering. Little changes. Petit. Piccolo. And happening over a l-o-n-g period of time.

We're not really changing that much... are we?

We might be aiming to change a lot of processes or systems and structures, or hell yes, let's change people, even just a few degrees would be great. Yet that is hard work. To get everyone - all of them - to shift. A little. All the teams, units and departments to all shift one or two degrees. That's a big deal.

Rather than tinkering on a little something with everyone, why not look at how you can truly transform a pocket, a division, a team, a squad or a unit. And dramatically. Markedly.

Pockets of transformation

Internal hubs, accelerators and pockets of innovative joy are popping up everywhere in cities, communities and businesses. Some companies are setting them up off-site in a cool warehouse-style environment, others are cordoning off a meeting room and labeling it 'The Innovation Lab' or 'hub' or 'foundry' or 'garage' or other mechanical-workshoppy-sounding noun where things are being furiously made.

Whatever you call your transformation pocket - and your business doesn't need to be large to do this - be sure to actually transform something... rather than tinkering with everything. Start there.

79

Do you major in minor or minor in major?

Jim Rohn's advice to avoid 'majoring in minor things' suggests we could avoid the large, unwieldy and lengthy change we're attempting to make to somethin' little. That can turn out to be a big mess.

There is a more helpful (diagonal) opposite. It's smarter, leaner and more agile to start with 'minoring in major things'. That is, carry out little experiments on some of the bigger things.

Then you can move step by step towards the big deal of majoring on those major transformative things.

(And the other distraction, that's minoring in minor things - ooh, it's all a bit scary so we don't do very much of anything at all. It's an area of big fear. We distract and procrastinate and confabulate and obfuscate.)

Too often the default change initiative is majoring in the minor. I think you need to keep a look out, and then get outta there.

It could look like this:

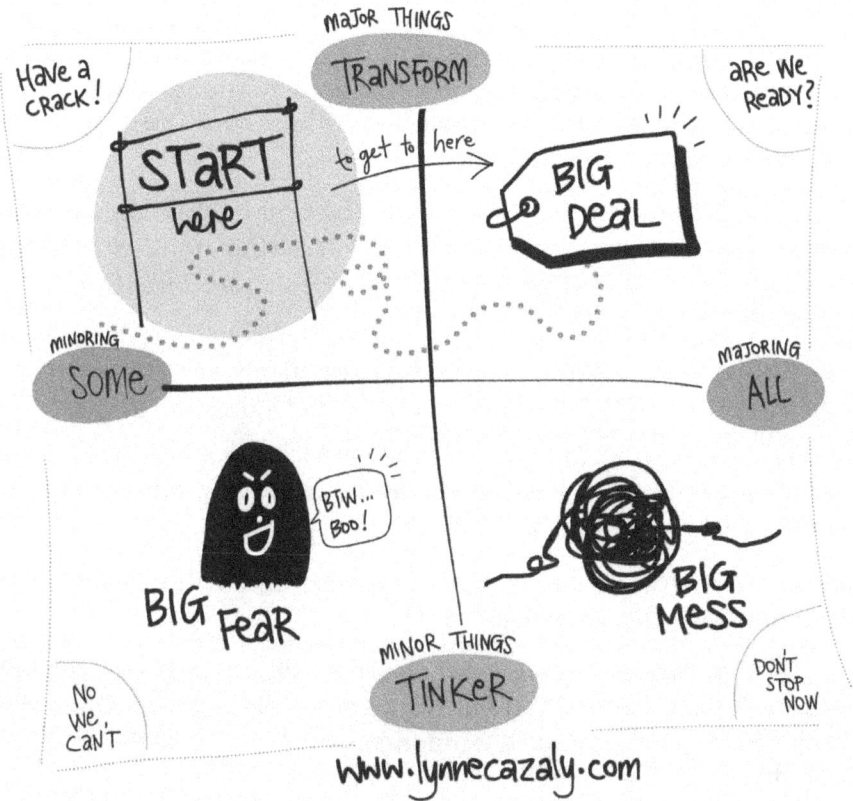

Where agility happens

So go ahead and 'have a crack' at radically changing something. This is where transformation is born. This is where success and practical failure live. It's way more experimental, experiential and insightful.

When you launch some experiments, you can see how they go. Then you can experiment faster, and get results faster and these will be results that are noticeable and reportable, applicable ... formidable.

You'll be playing a leaner game (a-la *The Lean Start-up*) with yes, perhaps a low-fidelity version of that something, but with insights and data that pour back to you way sooner than a long drawn-out change effort involving a cast of many and a calendar of many months... or years.

This approach schools us so that the next one we launch - if it turns out that it's actually worth launching another one or 'rolling' anything out to anyone - will be more efficient, more valuable and simply work better.

Leave those little barely there 'just noticeable differences' for the marketing world and their product packaging on supermarket shelves. They don't belong in change and transformation.

Don't fall into the safety of a too subtle, too gentle or too soft change - it keeps you busy but... it will do that for years. Yawn!

Too many people, projects, teams, units, industries and organisations are tinkering.

You can keep tapping away on a little bit of metal somewhere - tinker tinker - gently and fearfully at the edges of what could be great, hoping to make a few indents ... or you can melt the thing down, change it markedly (transform it) and see what new there is to work with.

It's minoring in major things, in transforming the some. This will help get you ready for bigger transformations up ahead. This is marked change and this is the type of transformation the world requires us to make today.

As Andy Noble and Eric Garton in the *Harvard Business Review* article *'How to make Agile work for the C-Suite'* state,

> *'To successfully transform to a more agile enterprise, companies must make conscious choices about where and how to become agile. They have to decide where to adopt agile principles and mindsets, where to use agile problem-solving methodologies to dynamically address strategic and organizational challenges, and*

where to more formally deploy the full agile model, including self-managed teams.'

If you wonder where to begin, who to start with, who to transform first... ahem, start at the top!

There is.. a no-regrets first move available to the leaders of organizations that are working through a complicated transition from a traditional to an agile enterprise, and that is to become agile at the top. Senior leadership teams that embrace agile do a few things differently.

- Eric Garton & Andy Noble

AGILE

Agile-ish

Why agile works

Short of being a literature review on agile or a summary of sources, there's plenty to read on the topic.

I enjoy the mini handbook *'Why agile works'* from InfoQ.

Because of this:

'Agile leaders are not only fast and effective problem solvers when dealing with situations they've never dealt with before, but they are also laser-focused on results and excellent at reshaping plans and priorities when faced with unexpected changes in the environment. They are resourceful and competitive. And, they get it done fast.'

According to the most recent *'State of Agile'* survey, agile has gone mainstream and the majority of organizations use agile techniques for at least some software development projects.

'We believe that if organizations adopt agile as a set of beliefs, they will develop an agile culture and that this agile culture is what leads to continuous adaptation and innovation. The focus of the change effort must be on the heart, not the head or the hands.'

And this...

'An agile culture, however, will continuously improve and adapt without the need for periodic change initiatives.'

The business of agility

At many an agile conference you'll find the Rally Software Development team folks (now owned by CA) with the blue book *'Agile Business: A leader's guide to harnessing complexity'*.

In the forward of the book, (which is a compilation of over 50 essays from different people in the field and authored by Bob Gower and Rally Software), Ryan Martens says it's a book of ideas:

- Build the right thing
- Build the thing right
- People not resources
- Agile steering and
- Transform your organisation.

After I'd received the book from Rally it sat on my bookshelf for awhile. As most books do. I think books then leap off the shelf and into our vision or into our hands at just the right time. As I read each page, I highlighted and underlined and found such clarity and simplicity. Particularly this one about 'It's the system':

'When we look around our businesses and see room for improvement, it's tempting to want to shake things up or change personnel. But if you look closer, you'll notice that the trouble is not the individuals but the system. Change the system and you'll change the behaviour.'

What we're really talking about here is business or organisational agility, the ability for a business to respond to change. And quick! And yes this will probably throw things into a state of chaos or confusion for awhile - all change processes do.

It's to shift from that stable, steady situation, into something that helps you respond to change and deliver better, greater value. Over time, if you respond to this change in a more agile-like way, you'll get better at it. It won't hurt as much and you'll make it part of what you just do.

The agile movement

Most contemporary references to agile are referring to the movement that has driven the software development industry over the past 15 or so years.

Other references are to panthers and cheetahs and other lithe and agile creatures!

But in the modern workplace, agile also gets bandied around like 'we need to be more agile' or 'this is an agile business' or 'our team is agile'.

Rather than obsessing over whether you are or not, know this: the software development industry and hundreds of thousands of people around the world have been following - as best they can - a bunch of principles and guidelines crafted in 2001 known as *The Agile Manifesto for Software Development*.

And here it is ...

Manifesto for Agile Software Development

We are uncovering better ways of developing software by doing it and helping others do it.

Through this work we have come to value:

Individuals and interactions over processes and tools

Working software over comprehensive documentation

Customer collaboration over contract negotiation

Responding to change over following a plan

That is, while there is value in the items on the right, we value the items on the left more.

Kent Beck

Arie van Bennekum

Ward Cunningham

James Grenning

Andrew Hunt

Jon Kern

Robert C. Martin

Ken Schwaber

Dave Thomas

Mike Beedle

Alistair Cockburn

Martin Fowler

Jim Highsmith

Ron Jeffries

Brian Marick

Steve Mellor

Jeff Sutherland

And those are the names of the men who crafted the manifesto.

At the Agile USA 2016 conference, the day before the five-day conference program, there was a full-day *Women in Agile* workshop.

Over 100 women in the room, representing the thousands of women who now call themselves part of the wider agile community. When the presenter Natalie Warnert kicked off the session, reporting on her research on women in agile, she showed that list of men's names as the signatories to the Agile Manifesto. And good on them for getting together and agreeing and crafting the manifesto.

And now women are part of it too. Very much a part of it.

Principles: Agile Manifesto

We follow these principles:

1. Our highest priority is to satisfy the customer through early and continuous delivery of valuable software.

2. Welcome changing requirements, even late in development. Agile processes harness change for the customer's competitive advantage.

3. Deliver working software frequently, from a couple of weeks to a couple of months, with a preference to the shorter timescale.

4. Business people and developers must work together daily throughout the project.

5. Build projects around motivated individuals. Give them the environment and support they need, and trust them to get the job done.

6. The most efficient and effective method of conveying information to and within a development team is face-to-face conversation.

7. Working software is the primary measure of progress.

8. Agile processes promote sustainable development. The sponsors, developers, and users should be able to maintain a constant pace indefinitely.

9. Continuous attention to technical excellence and good design enhances agility.

10. Simplicity--the art of maximizing the amount of work not done--is essential.

11. The best architectures, requirements, and designs emerge from self-organizing teams.

12. At regular intervals, the team reflects on how to become more effective, then tunes and adjusts its behavior accordingly.

Here's a visual of the Agile Manifesto I created a few years ago. I've found when speaking about things agile-ish, it helps to have something to talk to – beyond (and in addition to) the words of the Agile Manifesto.

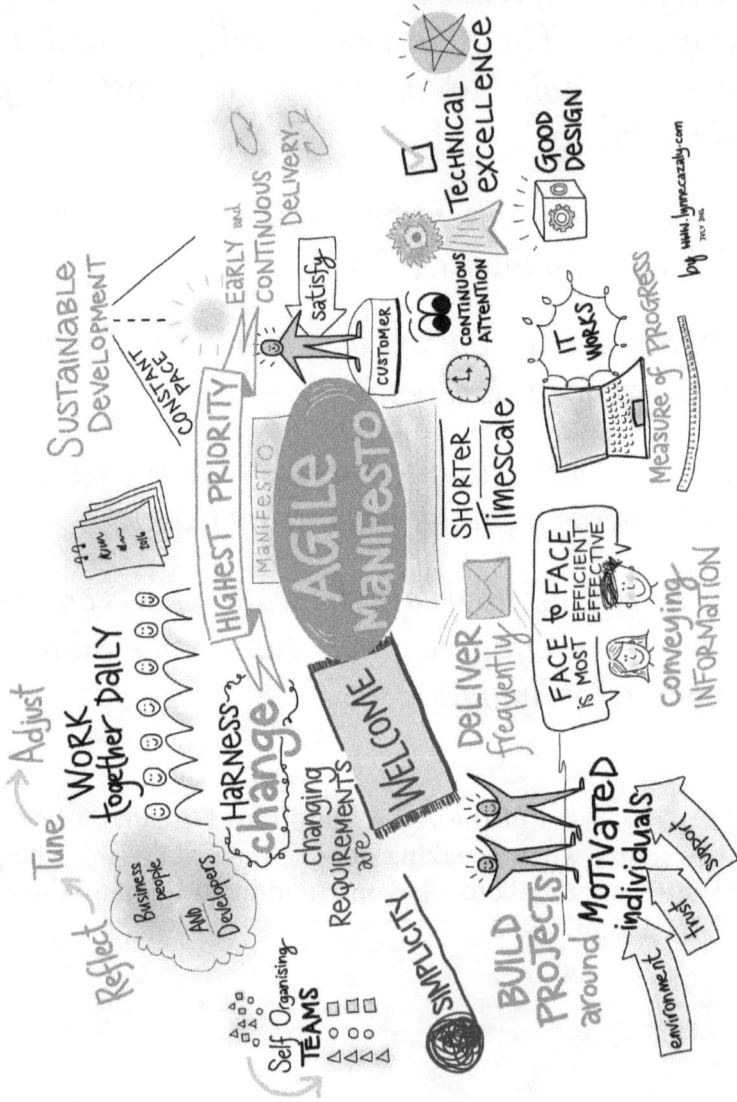

But will it work?

There are plenty of dissenters, debaters, haters and outspoken anti-campaigners on almost every topic you could think of: publisher published books vs. self publishing; private vs. public schooling; public transport vs. driving; bottled water vs. tap water; sparkling vs. still; owning vs. renting; married vs. defacto; one minute or two.

And so when there is a movement, a mass of people zigging, there will always always always be people who zag. They like to zag. They like to stand out, be different, voice their views. And that's great.

So here is what John Falcone on *'The Agile Times'* website (and people will have opinions about that, and about him) but here's the seven things he says people will have a problem with about agile. This might be helpful, you know, to help you stretch your own mindset so when/if you hear or see these sorts of things, you're ready to adapt. Not fight back, just listen, respond, do whatever an open mindset and agile-ish thinking person would do.

1. Focus on customers over shareholders

Hmm, now *this* might be different. Customer's first? What the? If the focus has been on shareholders this could be a huge shift in mindset. Delighting customers is it and a bit agile-ish.

2. Perceived loss of control

Can you imagine people running around organising themselves? How ludicrous! And what if they're managing themselves too? They might leave early or have 90 minutes for lunch and rip us off! And why do we need a manager anyway!?

Umm, you'll still need managers; it's likely that not everything will be agile-ish.

3. Perceived loss of authoritative rank and power

'Aye aye Captain' will be diminishing. It's all been so hierarchical that for any other shape - flat, networked, circular, random - could be freaky for some people. There will need to be some letting go and that is not easy to do. It's deeply embedded in many ageing company structures and won't shift with a simple decision to implement first thing Monday morning or on the 15th of next month.

4. Focus on delivering immediate customer value over immediate revenue

Shareholders need to be reported to and returned to. It's part of the equation of many businesses. And forecasts and predictions need to hold as firm as possible. Otherwise it's a bad look. Before you know it, the customer's needs may get pushed aside and the focus becomes *get that project done on time and on budget* or *in time for the quarterly profit reports*.

5. Too much learning and too much change

Once you're in a comfortable position of leadership in an organisation, it's easy to sit back. And when others are getting roles because of who they know and how many years they've clocked up, it's easy to think that learning and changing isn't required.

Some people won't like the items on the left of the manifesto.

6. Customer value is cumulative while overall benefits only come if done properly in the long run

The future is uncertain yet many companies don't realise that the longer-term value of a customer comes from...the longer term. When you have staff who are disengaged, they are often treated as a resource and terminated when they're not required. Plus it's a quick way to lower costs. It's all connected though. Remaining staff feel a lack of purpose and that flows on to the customer. There's a Richard Branson quote that seems to do the rounds: something about looking after your employees first because then they're more likely to look after your customers.

7. Increased level of transparency perceived as very risky

The trust is out there... or in here. And it's scary to share that stuff. Higher levels of transparency can equate to higher levels of fear for many. But while there are both positive and negative aspects that will be revealed in the increasing transparency of agile, the drive to avoid or reduce risk is strong. Trust diminishes, engagement plummets and it's all falling apart.

As you go through an agile-ish transformation – either for yourself, your team or the organisation and enterprise – there will be tricky spots and challenging times. It's the nature of working with people who are human and who have opinions and ideas.

I believe the best managers acknowledge and make room for what they do not know - not just because humanity is a virtue but because until one adopts that mindset, the most striking breakthroughs cannot occur. I believe that managers must loosen the controls, not tighten them. They must risk; they must trust the people they work with and strive to clear the path for them; and always, they must pay attention to and engage with anything that creates fear. Moreover, successful leaders embrace the reality that their models may be wrong or incomplete. Only when we admit what we don't know can we ever hope to learn it.

- Amy Wallace and Ed Catmull, Creativity Inc

Objections, complaints and whining

Some of the reasons why there might be objections, disagreements or thinking that an agile-ish culture ain't possible around here include:

- It won't work here. Flat out rejection. Just no.

Yes, you're right. It may not work. Depends on a few factors really, but a big one is what legacy have you got? How solid are those pillars of history holding up the joint? How complicated is the knitting? Yes, the knitting.

I was facilitating an innovation day with a team and one of the senior members of the team wasn't too keen talking about innovation; they feared it and then advised that we probably need to 'stick to our knitting', meaning to stay with the jumper we are currently working on! How dare we look to perhaps buy something ready-made or worse still, take up some other craft form.

Agile cultural transformations seem to work well for businesses that are open to what might be possible in the future. They have a willingness to adapt; they're still growing up and wondering what they want to be as they get older.

Other reasons or excuses include:

- It's too hard to change. Yes indeed it is hard. Needed, but hard.
- People are protecting their ass.
- Don't tell me what to do.
- Who wants to be wrong about this new thing anyway?
- Making mistakes is career limiting. Ah yes and so is doing nothing.
- Some of our business areas are trying it.

- It's only for tech and we're not tech. You might not be tech yet... wait a little while. You will be.
- It's for geeks and software dudes only.
- We've tried it before.
- Please give us the rollout plan for that.

Whatever the excuses, reasons and objections to agile, agility or even a little bit of agile-ish, you can be sure that not everyone will agree to everything.

But you've got to start something, somewhere.

Strong opinions about everything

We're human. You'll know how human we get when you have a group of people talking - think about a dinner party or a gathering of friends - and how the differences in opinions kick in.

It happens with parents and parenting; it happens with coaches and sports teams; it happens with chefs and cooking styles; it happens with car owners and their preferences for cars and radical views on other cars.

I had the joy of owning a BMW some years ago. The first brand new car I'd owned. Previously I'd been looking at a SAAB. I'd loved the look of their 95 model; the square back, the look of the lights; it all just said 'buy me' to me! And when I spoke to a motoring friend and expressed my desire about the SAAB he was able to shed some light on that exact make of car.

He said... *'There are two days when you're happy with a SAAB; the day you buy it and the day you sell it.'*

I couldn't believe it! How dare he diss this car that I'd researched and read about and drooled over and had photos on my dream and vision board about (no vision board, but I did have a SAAB brochure on my bookshelf with the cover facing out so I could see it and be inspired by it - call it a 'vision bookshelf' if you will).

So there he was, totally dissing my opinions and views and blatantly trashing this dream I had.

But it was simply his opinion. And it was my opinion too. And they were different. And that's a mindset thing. We had different points of view. Different perspectives. Different experiences and different ways of seeing things, that's all.

It's this different perspective that is so often the root of many arguments, wars, disagreements, break-ups and fights.

And we are too often caught up with pride and not being able to back down or see another view. This is what makes disagreements and arguments and wars so sad. This is how people have fallings out; this is how they never recover from the wrong done to them by someone else. It's a mindset difference. They thought one thing, you thought or believed another - the two are different, and there you have it.

And with agile-ish it will be no different.

Lynne Cazaly

AGILE -ISH

Agile-ish

Start Something

To start building a culture of agile or agility or agile-ish, you'll need to think a little differently and in turn, behave a little differently.

While it's such comfortable fun to stay the same, the future of work simply won't let us. The skills we'll need for 2020 and beyond are shaping up as a slick looking list!

The skill of having a design mindset – which is kind of agile-ish - is right up there. This doesn't mean you need to know your way around design software, or know which colours go with what or even what an industrial designer does.

Rather it's the frame of mind, the mindset that you adopt to think, solve and respond to what's going on in your team, business, and industry ... the world.

A same/same response is too ho-hum now. We can't do the same as we always have.

Businesses who need to adapt and thrive (that includes the solo operator right through to mega-global big name players) need to increasingly take a design approach to many parts of their business.

It's about making things your customers want, that deliver great value.

Get some momentum

Let's get moving. It's so much easier to keep going at speed and in flow and with greater success when you're already moving, than from a standing start.

Agile often has velocity or speed as a feature. You get going, get moving, get into flow. Get the team moving on something, rather than sitting around talking about perhaps one day working on something, maybe.

Momentum is important; just ask a kid on a swing.

As air traffic controllers and pilots know, momentum is everything... or nothing. I love listening to air traffic control and how advice on some days for departure at say, Runway 36 Left is to have a 'rolling start'. As a plane moves from the terminal, around the apron, onto the tarmac and then along the access roads that lead up to the runway, they'll receive the clearance from air traffic control to take off with a rolling start. That is, keep moving! You'll see them turn from the roadway, around the corner onto the runway and just keep the wheels moving, the engines begin revving and with the momentum of that massive beast loaded with tonnes of people, baggage, fuel and refreshments, momentum is everything. Keep moving. They turn the corner, onto the runway and then the engines receive full thrust and off they go, powering along the runway.

And given aircraft weight includes allowances for fuel for taxiing and take off, it's all part of the cost of flying.

You'll have to get moving on something to create a culture of agility.

Which one are you?

You were born with an agile or growth mindset – a way of thinking that says *'I can grow and learn and be challenged. I can improve.'* Think crawling, walking, talking, reading, riding a bike. So much to be challenged by.

But somewhere along the way, you might get derailed and think that you either 'have it' in this life or you don't. But that itself is a fixed mindset.

Linda Rising presenting at an Agile Singapore conference about an agile mindset was inspiring, relevant and ... a tap or slap on the shoulder. There are some vital characteristics that are required to make work work in today's competitive environment.

She said: *'who told you what you can and can't do'*... and she warned us to *'watch out what you're thinking'.*

An agile mindset is one that is looking for opportunities to grow, learn, experiment and improve. Failure simply gives us some information.

Carol Dweck's TED talk and book on growth mindset is a must see/must read on the topic of agile, agility and mindset too.

Our mindset need not be fixed; this mental agility is ideal for the volatile world we live in today. Our teams, customers, clients and organisations need us to be agile, flexible, adaptive, and responsive. It's through this type of challenge that we grow.

Look at where you might be fixed in your thinking. How might an agile mindset see it differently? What could you experiment with, test out or be challenged by? Go.... flex, bend, shift and grow. Keep challenging your own view of things.

The reasonable man adapts himself to the world; the unreasonable one persists in trying to adapt the world to himself.

- George Bernard Shaw

A Model of Agile-ish

If you want to be more agile-ish, there are some things you can start doing.

I'd rather not be too prescriptive by suggesting you do these things in this order and don't stop until you've done them. Rather, here are four things that I think make for an agile-ish team, unit, business, organisation.

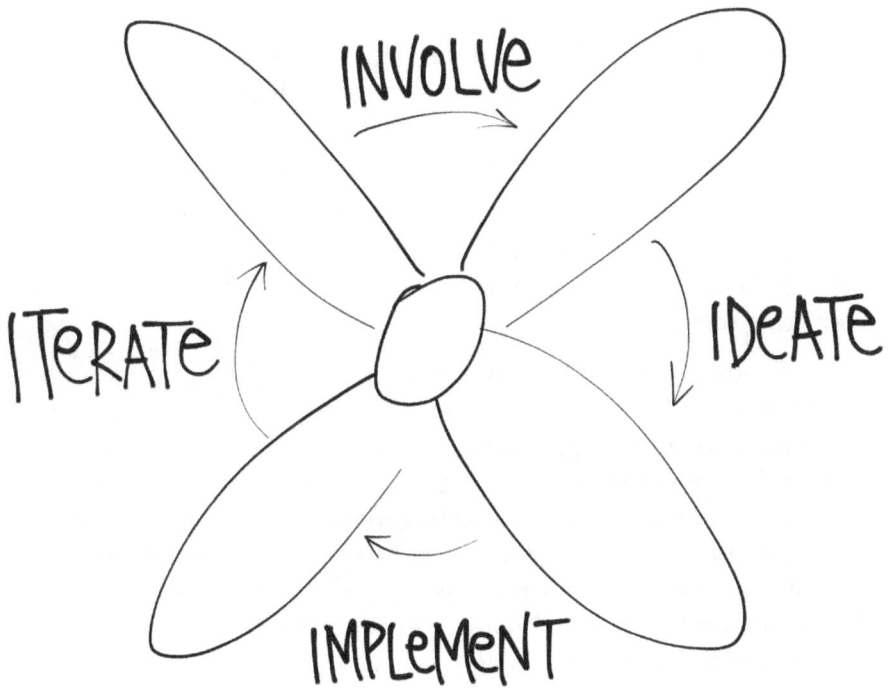

INVOLVE

ITERATE

IDEATE

IMPLEMENT

www.lynnecazaly.com

- Involve
- Ideate
- Implement
- Iterate

To deliver more value than you currently do, involve, ideate, implement, iterate.

And to do it quicker than you currently do, responding more swiftly, that to me is agile-ish.

Involve: it's about involving people, users, customers, colleagues. It means connecting more with people, not less. It's being closer to them and understanding more about who they are, what they need, what their problems and challenges are.

Ideate: this is about generating ideas and possibilities, solutions and answers and new ways of working, being and doing. It could be creating a new process or reducing how long the existing one takes.

When Australia Post looked at improving the time it took for a business to create a new online account, they were keen to reduce it from the previous 18 days to something a little more swift! By involving the team, users and customers and other parts of the business, they were able to generate other ideas and ways of getting the boxes ticked and the forms filled out. At the end of their lean-ish, agile-ish process, they'd been able to reduce that time of creating a new business account right down to two days. And that was a few years ago. I'm sure it's almost instantaneous now. Like most of our expectations, we want it now and Australia Post found a raft of ideas and ways to make that happen.

Implement: means putting the ideas, possibilities and solutions to work, putting them into practice. It's an experimental thing. It won't be perfect. It will be ish. This is where you need to welcome and accept failure. Don't put so much pressure on people that they're fearful of implementing things because they know they might not work perfectly. Relax the expectation. This is an experiment, it's a laboratory; let's see what happens.

Iterate: now we've run an experiment and have some results, responses, answers and information, we can tweak it. We can improve, adjust, add a bit here, remove a bit there and go again. We repeat it but with the insights of learning from the implement phase or stage.

Let's go to another layer and see what each of these phases is really all about.

Involve – is about empathy.

It's about connecting with people, understanding things from their perspective and seeing the truth of the situation or problem. You know you've experienced a lack of empathy from a friend or colleague – or a customer experience – where your view or experience just didn't register. They didn't seem to care or they didn't make you feel like they cared or knew what you were going through.

Ideate – is about creativity.

We may not think we're very creative but we're going to need to get over that mindset because we need ingenuity and innovation to generate possibilities. It's more than a clichéd brainstorming session in a dull meeting room. Contemporary creativity research identifies that boredom, daydreaming, walking, talking, reading, thinking and even showering are all good places to get ideas.

Implement – is about activity.

There is a point where we need to stop talking or stop planning and put something out there into the world. It's time to print, publish, ship, sell, test… whatever you need to do to spin the wheels on the thing. It can be a scary time because who knows what will happen next!

Iterate – is about agility.

Being quick to market is one thing; being quick to market with something that people want, love and use is a whole other thing. The best way to be agile-ish is to listen to and look at what happened when you implemented. Then make changes – big and small. Tweak and try it again. Improve and incrementally experiment. Again.

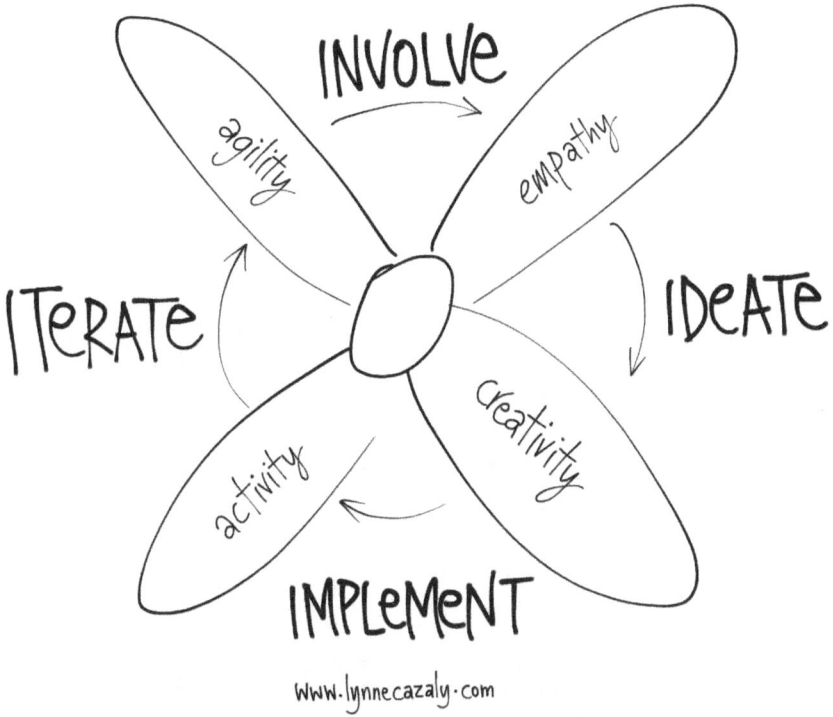

INVOLVE

agility

empathy

ITERATE

IDEATE

creativity

activity

IMPLEMENT

www.lynnecazaly.com

Empathy is a connection.
Ask and listen.

Ideas come from thinking.
Talk and think.

Implement is a verb.
Put it into practice.

Iteration is evolution.
Get ready to change.

- Lynne Cazaly

There is a flow or cycle to being agile-ish. I don't see it as overly prescriptive, rather it's suggestive. It's no box or grid that you must follow; it's no matrix that you need to fill the spaces of. It's a flow.

And you go around. By all means spend as long as you like on each. You might like to spend the next quarter just working on the first thing; and then tackle the others. Perhaps you'll look at the next thing when the team's ready. Or perhaps in that new role you're aiming for. Maybe it will be a clean start or clean break, a clean slate. Embracing the whole thing by next Tuesday may be a little high on expectations. You only have to be a little 'ish' at first.

As any leader, team or organisation creating a culture of agility will tell you, they are likely on a 'journey'. You might not remember when or where it started or how it started, but it started. They may not be able to show you exactly where they are but they are in some type of change... in a ceaseless transformation.

How might it not work?

Given the focus and interest of so many leaders and organisations aspiring towards some type of agility, on that journey there are often things that don't go to plan.

Perhaps we don't connect or involve our users or stakeholders, enough or in an ongoing way. Or we don't go deep enough. Or we think that them filling in a feedback from is enough. Nope, not enough. Not involved enough.

Maybe we don't want to be told by the people we supposedly serve that we need to change things or that we got it not quite right. It can mean more work and for some projects, the end of contracts or a change of focus. On other occasions it's about putting a stop to sunk costs. How far do you have to be down a path before you turn around, knowing it's the wrong path?

In many organisations we plan and plan and plan and plan. And we don't do anything. We have meetings to review the plan and the changes to the plan and a whole raft of people are working on this plan in this department but they're not actually doing anything. If we took them out of the business - which the business will have to do sooner or later because it's the very thing that's stopping them from being agile and responsive and adaptive, because they're busy planning – would we notice it if they were gone?

This happens time and again when a business that's returning lower than hoped results goes to slash and burn various departments. They tinker at the edges with a restructure and remove a bunch of people who are deemed to be no longer required.

Except that time a large financial institution cut the heart out of its business and removed thousands of mid-tier workers. All that was left were lower skilled teams who couldn't cope with the complexity and level of the work required to be done. There were plenty of 'people leaders' left who had no more people to lead. That company is still reeling and is trying to play catch up in the market by introducing new ways of working.

It might not work because we simply take too long to do anything. Not agile-ish enough.

Agile-ish

Lynne Cazaly

INVOLVE

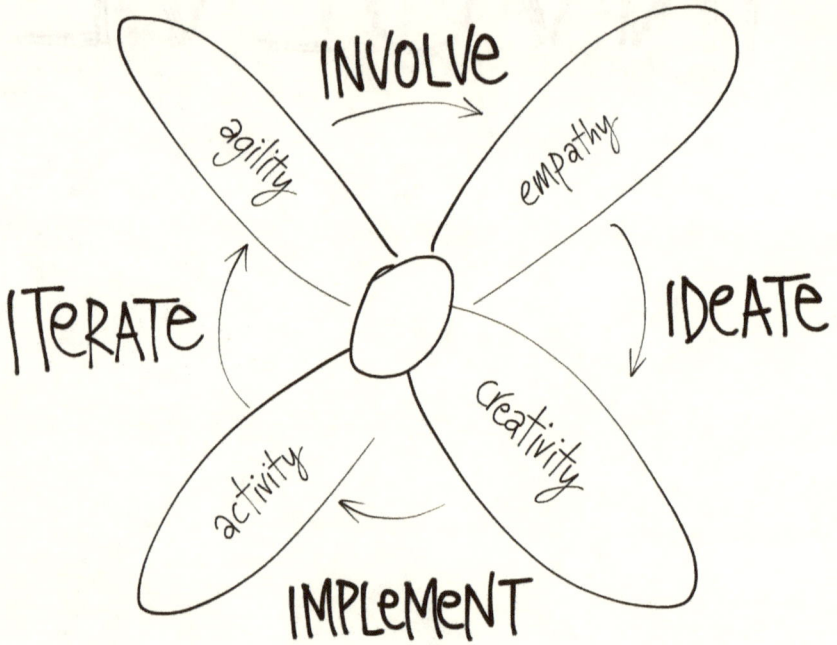

INVOLVE

agility

empathy

ITERATE

IDEATE

creativity

activity

IMPLEMENT

www.lynnecazaly.com

Get closer

Involving our users, customers and clients is not just about introducing the Net Promoter Score question:

How likely is it that you would recommend our company/product/service to a friend or colleague?

When we think about customers, users, clients... these might be the end users of your products or services, or the other teams, units and departments that you service or interact with in your organisation.

Often the 'internal customer' gets mocked or ignored or pushed down the list of priorities. But they're a customer nonetheless and their involvement can help you become more agile, more adaptive and more responsive. So while we're thinking about customers, clients... those sorts of people, think of them both right near you in a neighbouring department or team, as well as out there, on the other side of that window or the other side of the screen.

It's not just a 'tick the box happy sheet' in a training workshop. And it's not just asking customers to complete a feedback form at reception or staying on the line to give your customer contact staff a rating on how they went today.

Not just.

What if you followed your customers around?

What if you got closer to them - but not in a creepy way?

What if you actually involved them in the planning and design and delivery of services...?

As Martin Lindstrom says in his book 'Small Data', *there's a well-known quote that says if you want to understand how animals live, you don't go to the zoo, you go to the jungle.'*

What if you did what Lindstrom does - what if you 'moved in' with your customer? What would you notice? What would they tell you? How would it all work for them? I saw Lindstrom on a visit to Australia where he spoke at the striking Sydney Opera House. His presentation showed photographs, quotes and videos of some of the details of these customer interactions. He does kind of move in with them. At their place. He moves in with them so he can observe them and interact with them and get to know the intricacies of their behaviour.

His approaches are quite structured and defined and definite as he's observing and noting and watching.

As he says, *'My methods may be structured but they're also based on a whole lot of mistakes, and trial and error, and faulty hypotheses that I have to toss out before starting over again.'*

Aha, it seems Lindstrom himself has agility. He's made lots of mistakes, used a trial and error approach and had plenty of faulty hypotheses which he's ditched before going again.

But moving in with them? This might sound a bit drastic compared to how you're currently connecting and engaging with your customers and clients, but what if you took some steps towards this? What if you got a bit more involved? What if you got closer?

Lindstrom gets close. Why so close do you think? *'I look for patterns, parallels, correlations,'* he says, *'and, not least, imbalances and exaggerations. Typically I focus on the contrasts between people's day-to-day lives and their unacknowledged or unmet desires, evidence that can be found anywhere.'*

'A lone piece of small data is almost never meaningful enough to build a case or create a hypothesis, but blended with other insights and observations gathered from around the world, the data eventually comes together to create a solution that forms the foundation of a future brand or business.'

He goes on to say: 'After conducting what I call Subtext Research (Subtexting), a detailed process that involves visiting consumers in their homes, gathering small data offline and online, and crunching, or Small Mining, these clues with observations and insights taken from around the world, there almost always comes a moment where I uncover an unmet or unacknowledged desire that forms the foundation of a new brand, product innovation or business.'

All that travelling and observing. Isn't it a bit much? He says there are benefits. Among them is the ongoing opportunity to observe people and the cultures they inhabit from their perspectives, and to try to answer questions like:

- 'How do groups of people form?
- What are their core beliefs?
- What do they aspire to, and why?
- How do they create social ties?
- How does one culture differ from another?
- Do any of these local beliefs, habits or rituals have a universal significance?'

No matter how insignificant it first may appear, everything in life tells a story

- Martin Lindstrom

Get to know them

Those companies who connect, involve, engage and know their users, customers, patients and students are more agile. They are more likely to adapt. The greater the distance between you and your customers, the longer the message or opportunity will take to filter through to you. It just makes sense that a few more layers of people, processes and systems between customer experiences and you will take a while for things to soak through. If they ever do.

This is not to say that your customers, users, patients and students know what they want or that you should indeed build that or make that or sell that.

Leading design thinking business IDEO is globally recognised for matching what customers need and how to create something that works for them. In their online programs, their keynotes and their many resources, they are all about 'customer centricity'. And if this phrase hasn't reached the depths of your organisation's strategic plan or operational plan, insert that phrase now. And then work out how you're going to make the customer centric.

It's about creating a positive consumer experience at the pre, point of sale and post-sale.

It's such an opportunity to differentiate in a sea of beige.

You have to get closer to them. You're focused on them; you can't just say you're customer centric, you have to... be.

Complaining or connecting

It's easy to get frustrated with silly customers, annoying clients and frustrating users. Many a management consultant might cite the *BBC's 'Yes, Minister'* series and the episode about the hospital that ran efficiently, to budget and with no problems or issues. The hospital had no patients. Perfect hey? And while we might think that if they weren't there, or if they didn't muck up my day, or if they weren't rude or if they <insert other frustrating excuse about annoying person who buys your company's product or service> then everything would be well.

I guess this highlights our desire to make progress and get on with things. We don't like stuff slowing us down or getting in our way. So when an annoying customer gets in our way or slows things down, yes it can be frustrating.

But in the frustration and in your complaining is the most wonderful opportunity for connection.

- To find out why it's frustrating for you - or them.
- To find out more about the complaint.
- To find out what's happened and how we could fix it, remedy it, change it, rework it, rewire it, relaunch it, redesign it or rethink it.

The opportunity is absolutely right there.

Even in the darkest of moments or the most frustrating and annoying of situations, there's an opportunity to adapt and respond and be agile-ish about it.

It's something I've noticed when friends or family have moved suburbs or cities. They start off not knowing things, not feeling 'at home'. Of course not. They're somewhere else. But over time, once they've got to know their community and their community gets to know them, it becomes an opportunity of greater connection. Before long that new suburb or city is feeling familiar and you feel closer and more connected to it.

Listen out. Next time someone's delivering you an earful of complaint or next time you feel annoyed or frustrated because of a customer or client interaction, have a closer look. There is a big opportunity here to get closer, get more connected and more involved to really tease out what's going on and why it was a frustration.

There are many missed opportunities to make agile-ish responses and changes every day.

You can keep making lots of these types of changes to adapt and change a service. Don't wait for annual reviews or quarterly planning sessions or quality improvement meetings. Get together, identify the change, make the change, see how things go.

Build what they want

It's a bit mind reading-esque this getting closer to customers and users thing. From your involvement and engagement and discussions with them, you'll get greater insights into what it is that might work for them. You'll know more about what might work for them because you've got closer to them and you've stepped into their shoes.

For the teams at Metro Trains in Melbourne, getting information from customers is critically important. They use a number of ways to do this like focus groups, feedback sessions, a customer panel, feedback telephone number and another favourite technique I observed when working with their senior leadership team.

After a team forum one day - and before the after-event refreshments - senior staff headed out to the nearest train station with a handful of small palm-sized cards that were printed with a short message about customer service and engagement.

Staff headed down down down the escalators to the underground platforms, where customers were waiting for their trains. Then the most amazing thing happened: the leaders approached customers and engaged in a conversation! Yes, real customers. The leaders went right up to those customers and engaged in a conversation. They asked questions about the customer's travel, journey and experience that day and other days that week; what had worked, what didn't. Some staff started off a little hesitant to engage with customers – and this is understandable if there are reasons why you might get some angry or frustrated responses from customers. Plus, if you're not used to connecting with customers regularly, you might not know what to say. It may sound silly - how could you not talk to customers!!??

But for many people, it can feel uncomfortable or uncertain:

- will the customer respond or want to talk to me?
- do they have anything to say to me?
- what will I ask?
- what if I can't respond to their questions?

All of these fears and uncertainties of interacting with customers are normal. But once equipped with some conversation starters, the team got right into it. They all spent some time out there on the platforms and then came on back to the refreshments event, back at the forum venue. The stories they shared with each other were insightful, enlightening, uplifting, challenging, confronting... all of these things.

Most of all, they triggered situations that could be influenced by the team. Immediately they were looking for ways to respond and adapt, to be more agile-ish, to change what they could change.

It was thrilling then at the next forum in 90 days time to hear what staff had done to respond to the things customers had given in those initial conversations. Changes had been made across many areas of the business and a number of new projects and initiatives had commenced on larger changes, that would take more than a sign off or the flick of a switch.

In all my dealings with Metro Trains Melbourne, I found leaders who were willing to hear and willing to listen and willing to be closer to customers.

One manager in particular, Brad Voss, in the customer experience area reveled in customer conversations and getting closer to understanding them, meeting them, talking to them, finding out what they wanted or what they were challenged by. His enthusiasm was always infectious and optimistic. Some people they either fear customer interactions or worry the ongoing conversations about challenges or negativity might beat them down over time. But not Brad. Always thinking of what's possible, what do customers need, how do we make this the most wonderful experience for them and what else could we be doing to adapt and change and be more agile. Every interaction was an opportunity to find out more.

As the song 'Getting to Know You' from the classic 1951 Rodgers and Hammerstein musical 'The King and I' sings, 'Getting to know you/Getting to know all about you/Getting to like you /Getting to hope you like me.' Sung by the character Anna in the musical, it was about getting to know the many wives and children of the King of Siam. Yes, that's some serious getting to know you. But it's this closeness, the understanding and a greater empathy for that other person that helps build a connection and keep that connection.

There's an opportunity to see customers like places and people we can get to know, not be annoyed by. Admittedly, yes some experiences in customer service are highly frustrating and challenging.

A colleague who is a health care retailer sometimes speaks of the challenges of dealing with rude customers or customers who seem to have lost their ability to simply engage in a polite and human way.

Given the pressures of illness, healthcare, the effects of some medication and the challenges of dealing with life in general, it's no wonder customer interactions can be tricky, challenging frustrating.

While there is no silver bullet to fix every customer interaction, it's about getting closer to them to find out what's going on for them. Indeed, it's in the moments of high frustration or anger or dummy spits where something isn't working that reveals great opportunity. Indeed, people may be rude, but there is something else here; an opportunity to communicate better, deliver better, change a system or process so that staff can respond and adapt. That is also agility.

There are internal customers too. This includes customers across a business - not just outside or on the other side of your website or contact centre. Get to know them too.

A contracting gig earlier in my career where I helped develop communication materials for a department in a global firm comes to mind. In the early days of this contract, I didn't sit at my desk; I got out and talked to the people in that department. Every day I was meeting people, sometimes over coffee or lunch or simply dropping by their work area to learn more about them and the goals they had and the challenges they were working to address.

I recall ~~being scoffed at~~ receiving feedback like, *'Gee, when are you going to 'get on with it'?*

In fact I *was* getting on with it! This is how vital the phase of involve is and how misunderstood or undervalued it often is. I was getting on with it; I was deep in it already and the successful outcome of the programs and work were due to knowing what was going on for the client.

Agility is all about grace-under-fire and having a capacity to move quickly and decisively in anticipating and taking advantage of opportunity, whilst collaborating to avoid negative and even catastrophic consequences of change.

- Stephen Scott Johnson

How involved do you want people to be?

As you go further into the 'involve' aspect of agility, think about **how involved** you want customers, users, clients to be.

There's involved and then there's... INVOLVED.

You may want them just informed about what you want to do or perhaps ask them a few questions, or go further to having them have a greater say in what you do and how you do it.

When I'm working with businesses that are trying to get closer to their customers, I have them work through a gauge or scale of public participation from IAP2 - the International Association of Public Participation.

At each stage, you can ask questions like:

- Is this a briefing or transfer of information? (inform)
- Is it a consultative thing: I want to ask some questions and find out what they think? (consult)
- Do I need to involve them in the design or development of a process, product or service? (involve) - aha, now we are getting somewhere.
- Is it about collaboration: 'let's work on this thing together'. (collaborate)
- Do I want them to pick up the ball and run with it, to leave it to them so that they act and decide? (empower)

Whichever or how many of these you'd like to make happen – and you may want to achieve several on one piece of work - you need to be clear, otherwise it can get awkward and time wasting for all parties.

I like to think of it as deep sea diving or scuba diving - versus floating and snorkeling on the surface. Put your dive mask on: how low do you wanna go?

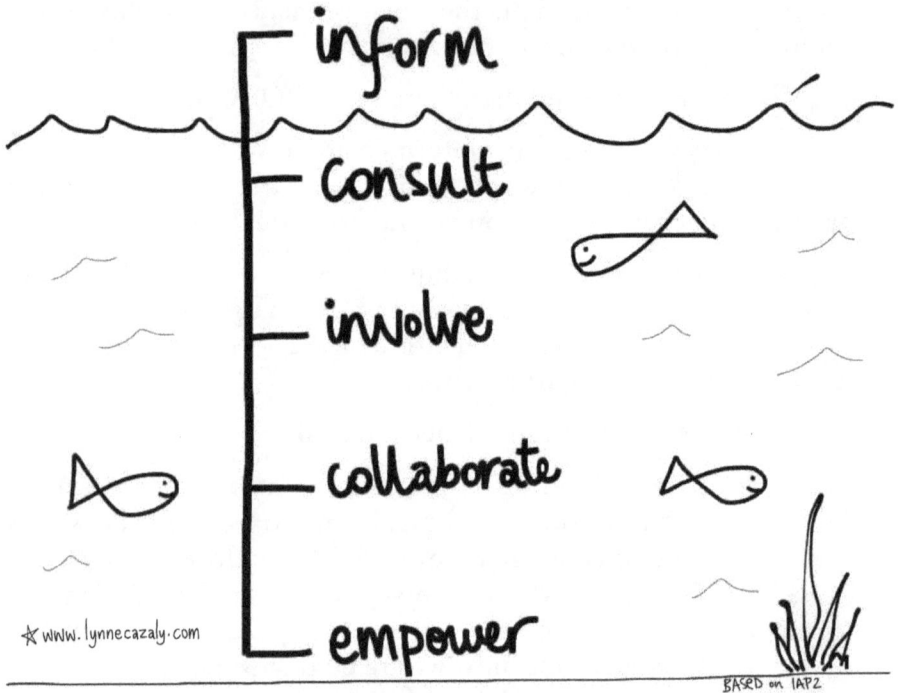

★ www.lynnecazaly.com

BASED on IAP2

Let's start at the top, on the surface, swimming around on some beautiful crystal turquoise water out in the Pacific Ocean somewhere:

Informing people about things is very much on the surface. You tell them, they listen. That's it. It's information. I think this is traditionally what companies and businesses have done for decades. Think of the banking sector; they dished out money and you followed their processes. Healthcare: you showed up and they did the procedure. Travel agents: you went to the shop and they sold you a trip on a ship cruise.

As the customer increasingly becomes at the centre of things, just informing doesn't cut it anymore. People want more.

So you can go further.

When you **consult** with people, you're getting under the surface, you're asking them what they think. You want their views and those views may well impact the shape and size of things to come.

This could be like focus groups. You gather people in a room, ask them some questions, listen to what they have to say but you may not do anything with that information. Conversely you may take every word down, analyse it all and make sweeping changes based on what you've gathered.

I'm an aviation geek and love flying my homeland's airline, Qantas. One of the safest airlines in the world. I love being on the Qantas Panel, their regular communication with regular flyers. A few hours after I land in my destination I'll receive an email from them asking *'How was Qantas?'* The link goes through to a series of questions and rating scales.

And yes, it begins with the standard Net Promoter Score question - the global scale that measures satisfaction and refer-ability - *'how likely are you to recommend our service to friends and colleagues'* - or similar. From there Qantas tracks through all stages of arriving at the airport, checking in and if I had an interaction with staff there; then on to whether I used the airport terminal facilities, whether I used the lounges and what I thought of them, then onboard the plane and how that went, through to arrival at my destination, plus luggage and baggage services and the entire arrival experience.

It makes me think back through the whole experience. I enjoy providing insights, praise and feedback on the things that went well and suggestions and comments for the things that didn't work so well.

Imagine all of this data, combined with all of the data from all of their other panel members responding after every flight.

This is consulting with your users.

Yet you can go further.

To go deeper is to **involve** people. How do they see things? What would they do? What do they think needs to happen? Get their ideas, their thoughts, their ways of thinking and seeing and bring them into the situation. I love to work with clients who go deeper and involve their customers. This means being alongside them as they use their product or service, interacting during the process and discussing and learning so very much from the customer.

If you were a bus company you might ride with your customer. If you're a health care provider, you'd walk through the service and experience with them; if it were Qantas they might pick me up at home and talk with me the whole way of getting to the airport and going to my destination. Sure this takes resources but it gives you what Martin Lindstrom calls *'Small Data'*. These intricate pieces of information could unlock an absolute game changing competitive advantage or customer delight so huge it becomes a profitable and highly successful lever for the organisation to pull ...and for customers and users to enjoy.

And, yes you can go further!

To **collaborate** with people, you go deeper. 'Co' means together. Now you're talking, listening, meeting, co-creating, co-designing and co-delivering this thing together. Regularly. Often.

I think this phase can worry a few leaders and managers. They may have it already set in their mind what they're going to do with a particular project or piece of work. But that's not an agile-ish mindset. That's a fixed mindset. Perhaps we resent having to make lots of changed. Oh it's so much hard work!

If we've invested significant time into something - the sunk costs become a big barrier to change. Who wants to hang up on a customer service call when you've already spent 45 minutes waiting? You'll lose your place in the queue and have to do it all again at another time! So there's that fear that 'all the work we've put into this' might be lost. That's right. It might. It might be 'wrong' or irrelevant for customers. That might mean you've wasted your time working on something.

But this is the whole point: o deliver things that are of value to your clients and users; which in turn are of value to your business because you'll be working on the stuff that delivers value, not wasting time working on the wrong things.

And you can go even further - you can go where people are **empowered** to design, create, deliver or implement a change or project. Give them power, decision-making, financial, resources, timing: it's theirs for the making.

I regularly use these five levels and depths of involvement and participation to guide my clients in working with their clients and customers.

Just as a trained scuba diver plans their dive, maps out the use of their oxygen supplies and prepares their equipment, companies too need to plan the depth of involvement and engagement with the customers and users.

So are you feelin' it? Empathy, that is.

As Jon Kolko says in the book 'Well Designed: How to use empathy to create products people love',

'the design process... leads to innovation and emotionally engaging new products and services. This process is centred around empathy and is built on deep research with real people in their natural environments'.

He goes on to answer how we can gain such empathy because 'to understand and design..for emotional appeal, it's critical not only to understand people, but to truly empathise with them in order to feel what they feel. How can you gain such empathy? The only way is by spending time with people and getting to know them on a personal and intimate level doing your best to see what they see and experience what they experience'.

Of course the whole approach to getting closer to customers and watching, observing and more deeply understanding them is all about gaining insights.

Insight is connected to intuition, about grasping the inner nature of things in a more intuitive way. It's about getting a clearer or deeper perception and understanding of a situation. Often it's like a light has been switched on or shone on to something. I think it's why the light bulb image or icon has so often been associated with innovation and ideas and creativity.

The 'a-ha' is the switching on of insight; a blinding flash of light. It's a revelation or a breakthrough. A flash of understanding. Perhaps there's no coincidence that in the exploration of the planet Mars, one of the robotic landers is called *InSight*. (I've had a crush on the *Curiosity* rover for years!)

Kalko continues on to say that insight is a *'hypothesised guess about human behaviour, but framed as a definitive truth'.*

Whatever the definition, it's clear that insights are a portal or pathway to innovation and a must in a business that's seeking agility.

Kolko later explains that getting those behavioural insights from customers and users is imagining it as a dialogue - the dialogue though is happening between the customer and your product or service. It may be an abstract kind of conversation but it's that kind of interaction. This is what makes human behaviour. Kolko says that gaining this behavioural insight involves spending *'time with the people who are going to use your product and watch them do whatever it is they do.'*

And further, *'your goal is to both understand them and empathise with them. You can accomplish this by absorbing and interpreting signals... (that) are local, discrete and specific.'*

Sounds similar to Martin Lindstom's view on *'Small Data'.*

Empathy is more than just stepping into someone's shoes - which is the apt and often quoted explanation of empathy. Kolko says it *'is about acquiring feelings. The goal is to feel what it's like to be another person'.*

Can ya feel it? Not just think it but feel it too?

Importantly it can help to be in the place where the behaviour actually happens. Kolko suggests *'you need to watch the behaviour happen. And you need to talk to the people who are doing it. That's all there is to it. ...You simply have a conversation with someone, while (they) perform some sort of activity or takes some action.'*

Once you get over a little awkwardness - like some of the Metro team may have felt in my earlier story about engaging with train customers - that can come up from conversations with strangers, you'll find it gets 'on a roll' and gives you plenty of priceless insights.

I find this every time - every time - I facilitate a workshop with a client. I'm often presented with a room of strangers; I might know a couple of people from some of the initial conversations and briefing but when it comes to the day or program of work, often I'm having to work immediately with strangers.

But the thing is, people are asked so infrequently for their opinion -- usually they're trying to fight to be heard! They're talked over and interrupted and mansplained to and cut off -- or not even given the chance to contribute. So you asking them some questions and getting their conversation going to gain insights will be a super opportunity - for you and them!

Don't let anything they say or do get away from you. I make sure I take copious notes or I'll use Voice Memo on my phone to record the interaction - with their permission - or I'll set up Garage Band to record on my laptop or I'll have a digital recorder. In many cases I'll use them all - always keen to back up the back up.

Then the file goes off to Rev.com for the first pass at the transcription. Their automated processes are pretty good, getting fairly good capture of content - including tricky Australian accents - and the background noises or the challenge of multiple voices getting fired up about something! With the first transcription done, I then have my Business Manager, Myra listen to it and make any corrections to the transcription and then I listen back and read the transcription. It's like reading a script while you're watching a film. (Have you done that before? Found the script online for a film and then watched the film and followed the script. Hours of fun!)

There's much more to read and explore on the topic of empathy and how it sits as a strong framework for making great decisions and achieving business agility.

Clearly I'm a fan of Jon Kolko's work along with others I've listed in the References section. Deep Patel in the article *'10 Ways*

Leaders Can Better Connect With Their Customers', curiously suggests these 10 ways!

'1. Social media posts

2. Blog posts

3. Responding on Quora (a question and answer site where questions are answered by the community)

4. Using chat software

5. Doing community service or outreach

6. Holding an 'Ask me anything' session

7. Hosting events

8. Having feedback sessions

9. Being transparent in how people can reach you

10. Responding to criticisms and comments openly.'

Why not join some customer panels yourself or sign up and attend some focus groups or customer engagement or consultation sessions so you can observe how companies connect with you and involve you. Or don't involve you! It can be enlightening to notice what they're missing. What are they missing?

Get the experience as a customer first, then think about how you could apply that to your company's customers.

Agile-ish

Lynne Cazaly

IDEATE

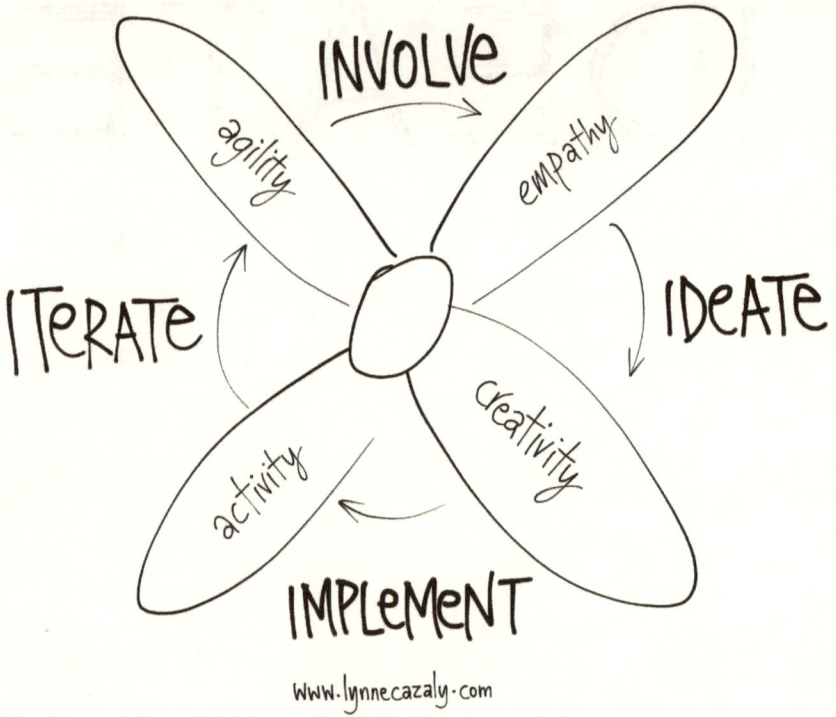

INVOLVE

agility

empathy

ITERATE

IDEATE

creativity

activity

IMPLEMENT

www.lynnecazaly.com

Is this about creativity?

If this stage of Ideate is about creativity then I'm sure there are plenty of people trotting out the *'I'm not that creative'* excuse. Along with the *'I can't draw'*, *'I can't cook'* and other dismissive *'I cant's!'*

Yet wherever you are in life, creativity is a must. It's a survival skill! The World Economic Forum and other predictors of skills we need to survive the brutal future are forever putting creativity somewhere in the list of the Top 10 skills.

You can't ignore the powerful force of ingenuity, creativity, the cleverness of us humans to make up stuff and then apply it to solve tricky conundrums.

If the thought of coming up with ideas and doing anything creative-ish fills you with dread, then fear not. It's not a game of creativity or who can make the prettiest thing; it's more a game of adaptability and who can put something out there that might be valued.

If you try to make something that everyone will love and adore, you'll be at it for a long time. You'll never get there in fact. So it's best to come up with a bunch of ideas and put them out there ... which we'll do in the next phase of agile-ish.

But for now, this is about ideas.

Ideation is a term that seems to have landed in many a business setting probably because it sounds more important than 'idea'. Ideation somehow becomes a silly verb. It simply means *'the process of forming and relating ideas'* - it's a noun and I looked that up just now on the Dictionary app on my iPhone. I could have referenced it all properly but this is 'ish' territory remember and one definition from an app is good enough for me to go with. This isn't a dissertation or thesis.

Ideate means more of a metaphysical thing; the actual existence of an idea.

But I like it as a verb - of coming up with ideas, bringing them into reality. You can't just have an idea in your head and leave it there. Well yes you can; we've all had plenty of ideas we haven't acted on. But in the case of agile-ish, I think ideas have to get into some type of action – even if it's just running it by some of your customers and users.

The verb ideate is to imagine, conceive of, envisage. What a wonderful thought. You *form a mental image of something that isn't present or isn't the case.'*

It all stems from Latin: 'ideatum'.
Which means idea.

An idea is a 'personal view'; it's an opinion or sentiment. It's the 'content of cognition', the contents of your thoughts, the 'main thing you are thinking about'. It could be a concept or a plan, a program or a figment, a suggestion or impression or a feeling. It could only be a whim or a hunch or it could be something more meaningful and with more substance. It could be a theme, a motif, a kink or something of inspiration.

It's connected to your mind; something you have in your mind, a purpose or intent. It's from Latin and Ancient Greek - a notion or a pattern.

And you never know where an idea may lead you.

The key is to not let it stay in your mind as a hunch or whim or idea. It's vital to get the idea and thinking out, into reality. It's a little like steam, to water, to ice. They're such different forms. You can't ice skate on steam, you can't make creases go away on a shirt using ice – or can you? Please try it out, experiment, and report back to me would you? But each form has their own use and application. The same with ideas; in your head they are in one form, steam, if you like. Bring them to water, make them something so they can be used, consumed, seen, absorbed. Ice is another form, another use, and another application.

Every once in a while, a new technology, an old problem, and a big idea turn into an innovation.

- Dean Kamen

Ideas are your only currency

So says the wonderfully clever Rod Judkins in his book of the same name, '*Ideas are your only currency*'. In a world where likes and shares and programs and Netflix take our time, we've got to realise they are all the result of ideas. Ideas that someone had, they created and put them out into the world. Ideas: our ability to make and create them is an incredible human ability. We all have it.

None of this, 'I'm not creative' bullsh*t ok?

Judkins in his book proposes 100 creative projects to open your mind and inspire great ideas. There are blank spaces where you can add to his suggestions, thought starters, outlines and templates. And he poses questions to get you going on those creative things. He really is challenging us to work through activities that prove to us that indeed we are creative and we can come up with ideas.

It's just that so many awfully boring meetings we've attended have made us doubt otherwise.

So many articles in *Harvard Business Review, Forbes, Inc, Entrepreneur, Fast Company* and *Wired* will give you tips on how to come up with ideas. Most mornings when I check out my feed curated through Flipboard there they are; lists on how to come up with ideas. So many, I've included a list of my favourites below. These work for me just fine. You might be different and know that you are; or you might be open to finding and working with some ways that you haven't tried before.

We are much more creative than we allow ourselves to be.

For example, if I asked you where you'd love to holiday, where would you go? How would you like to travel there? What would you like to do when you first arrived there? What would you do as a tourist escape or activity on the second day? And what type of food would you like to try during the trip? Is there a full day's mega-program you could imagine setting up, a kind of itinerary on steroids for one of the most memorable days? What would that look like? What would be in it?

There. If you've done that you've been creative. You've imagined and generated and created and crafted and wondered. You most likely pictured things in your mind and hopefully got a little excited about the possibilities you were creating. This *is* creativity.

Some ways to ideate

1. List 10 possible uses or applications of the thing.

2. Answer 'How would Richard Branson solve it?'

3. What would Helen Mirren's advice be?

4. How might a baker work on this?

5. What's the bigger problem or issue this is part of?

6. How could it become a game?

7. What would an avant-garde fashion designer do?

8. Pick up a random book from a shelf and open it at page 48. What does it say in there?

9. Listen to a piece of music to fire up your creative juices.

10. Go for a walk.

11. Take a shower.

12. Get bored.

13. Doodle and draw.

14. Read something else – on an entirely different topic.

15. Have a nap and awake with an idea.

16. Stare or meditate.

17. Pick up a completely different magazine than what you'd normally read. Get some inspiration there.

18. Write down two words – any words - and link them.

19. Look out a window - what do you see? Write it all down.

20. Get three people together to talk about it. Boom!

Doing these types of activities stimulates our thinking. Ignore the boring brainstorming around-the-room technique in dull meetings. You've got to inject something else and these methods are proven techniques to get ideas brewing.

Map the thinking

More and more industries and workplaces are demanding we be more innovative, creative, critical thinkers. With that in mind and if failure is sexy, that means we have a world of people who are keen – and needed - to keep looking around, wondering, improving and trying stuff out. They're being creative and can be our guides to greater creativity.

I reckon that might be you.

I'm giving a big shout out and encouraging thanks to the:

- **adventurers** : the people who cringe at bureaucratic BS and wasteful systems;
- **modern day mapmakers and cartographers:** who help people see what's going on and where we're going; and
- **toolsmiths:** those who use any type of tech, digital or analogue tool or implement to get sh*t done.

You're important mavens, facilitators and creative thinking connectors in the workplaces of today ... and the future.

I think we're always on the dangerous edge of losing touch with each other or wasting time on activities that don't really make a difference. I particularly want to zoom in on the mapmaker, the cartographer who helps guide or map what the heck is going on. They are the legends of productivity and often they don't realise it.

Maps unlock and formulate meaning

Static maps of two dimensional things – locations, objects, the universe, stars and planets – have a history as old as time. More recently, 3D and interactive maps have given us more knowledge, awareness, access and opportunity.

We're able to depict so much information and detail on a map, thanks to (now) well-recognised symbols and icons. And with the rise of digital mapping on our phones and devices, I think we're breeding a new generation of map lovin' people; who either like checking out (or in) where they are, or would LOVE to see more about where things are heading on your project.

But there's more to maps than just using them on our phones or devices to find out where we are or to use a GPS in a car to plot out the best or most scenic route.

Maps have a stunning place and role to play in the workplace and in the formation of ideas and creative thinking.

Here's how you can link maps to creativity:

Start by mapping the dialogue

Dialogue mapping is the activity of facilitating a conversation and capturing the threads. When people say stuff, you write some of it down. It's that easy.

Once you've got some threads, you write 'em down. These threads I'm talking about, it's what we mean when we say 'connecting the dots'. Often you'll hear people ask, 'Does that make sense?' They're hoping you're connecting the dots!

It's known as sense making: we're trying to work out what's going on and what we need to do about it. Often these phrases, comments and threads are the origins of creativity.

The beauty of a dialogue map is that you don't let key content vaporise upward in the room back out through the air vents! No, you capture it and map it. It means others can see what is being said, in dialogue. It brings seemingly unrelated items together, creating a systems approach to thinking, ideas and conversations.

A map does not just chart, it unlocks and formulates meaning; it forms bridges between here and there, between disparate ideas that we did not know were previously connected.

- From The Selected Works of T.S. Spivet by Reif Larsen

But map what?

If you're wondering what you would put on a map, try some of these:

- For competing sides use an argument map or a pros and cons chart
- Isolate the questions people have or are asking
- Collate the ideas you're coming up with
- Scope out the rationale
- Pinpoint the data, sources of information or research
- Show the connections and relationships, links and lines.

Yes, these are all maps.

The land was unknown before you mapped it and now there's a map, there's a way forward.

You'll look like an adventurer, even if you don't feel like it because that map helps keep holding the threads of ideas together.

I've found dialogue mapping to be one of the most powerful tools working with groups and different cultures, countries, fields, industries, levels of literacy and in groups of large and small numbers.

It helps spark creativity and helps generate new options, possibilities and solutions. It's most certainly an ideation tool and you can be creative without needing to be arty.

'Hooray!' is what people often say (out loud or in their head; you can tell by their a-ha facial expressions!) when they see the product or thing you're discussing taking shape. They're finally able to see what's been sitting quietly in other people's heads!

Then once it's up there, further collaboration happens. You can keep building on it.

Beyond that conversation or meeting, it becomes an artifact of the conversation; it marks a time in history when ideas were captured and sense was made based on what was known. Anyway, maps keep getting revised all the time! This may be version I. They're 'ish' too!

We are not listening all the time

Mapping the dialogue helps people hear each other's ideas. Because we're not really listening, are we? Hello? Are we? Well not ALL the time! I don't think it's about 'making' people listen to us, rather we need to use some other ways of making information

- easier to relate to (what's in it for me)
- quicker to digest (who's got time for big hefty packs of information)
- clearer to understand (we're all important here).

This isn't about dumbing anything down. We are always going to have complex information and content to deal with.

But we must try a little harder to be better sense makers - for creative capturers and others in the room and most importantly, for those who aren't in the room!

Dialogue mapping helps people hear what's being said that they just missed (while they were checking their phone).

It helps capture complex content and represents the views of all, not just the loudest.

It helps create shared understanding and it helps track or capture lots of ideas and trains of thought, not just the 'winning idea'.

Meetings end up being shorter, more gets done, it's a richer experience and it's highly engaging. Your brain cannot look away (for too long) when there is a changing map up there on the wall, whiteboard, window or chart.

If you're stressing thinking this is art...

Please relax. It doesn't really matter what your map looks like; it can have roads and cities and stops marked on it like a real road map or subway map for example; or it could be a bunch of circles connected with lines or perhaps one wavy line with some points marked on it or a few cloud-blob shapes with some words in them.

In the words of Sensemaking guru Karl Weick...'*any old map will do*'. It doesn't matter what it looks like, ok? Just have something for people to look at so they know where they are and what's going on. If you're thinking it has to be arty-creative... no.

But not too box-y. I would put one rider on maps; I think there is a danger in having a boxy organisation chart-style map that we've lovingly created on our desktop in PowerPoint over the past three days. Urgh. If it looks like a hierarchy or control-like or template-ish, no, it's not a map.

We can get a little hung up on trying to make a 'plan on a page' and then reducing all that text down to six point font size so it fits in all the boxes we've jammed on the page. In trying to make sense we've gone all box-ey. That's an over-engineered piece of vanilla that neither engages nor inspires people to be generative with ideas. It might tick somebody's box but it's not going to light anyone up with 'hey, that looks amazing; let's work on this thing'.

Then. Now. Next

The main thing to do is create something that helps people see: where they are and where you're all going. Capture the ideas and hunches as they come.

Then you've got something to go with; you can start working out how you'll get there. Road trip anyone?

To put a city in a book, to
put the world on one sheet of
paper -- maps are the most
condensed humanized spaces
of all... They make the
landscape fit indoors, make
us masters of sights we can't
see and spaces we can't
cover.

- Robert Harbison from
'Eccentric Spaces'

Hubs, Clubs and Havens

If you need to create a safe creative space whether it's an incubator or accelerator or a meeting room or some type of hub that's a space for this 'new world' you're creating, go for it.

In the *Harvard Business Review* article *'Changing Company Culture Requires a Movement, Not a Mandate'*, Bryan Walker and Sarah A Soule, suggest that we create safe havens.

They say, *'movement makers are experts at creating or identifying spaces within which movement members can craft strategy and discuss tactics. Such spaces have included beauty shops in the Southern U.S. during the civil rights movement, Quaker work camps in the 1960s and 1970s, the Seneca Women's Encampment of the 1980s and early 1990s. These are spaces where the rules of engagement and behaviors of activists are different from those of the dominant culture. They're microcosms of what the movement hopes will become the future.'*

Translating that into the workplace, the contemporary business world, these might be a meeting room that's labeled 'The Factory' or 'Lab' or 'Foundry' or other industrially creative label that suggests 'stuff is being changed or forged or made here'.

The authors go on to say, *'if your hope is for individuals to act differently, it helps to change their surrounding conditions to be more supportive of the new behaviors, particularly when they are antithetical to the dominant culture.'*

Yes you'll have to do something potentially new and different to support the team in doing something new and different.

IMPLEMENT

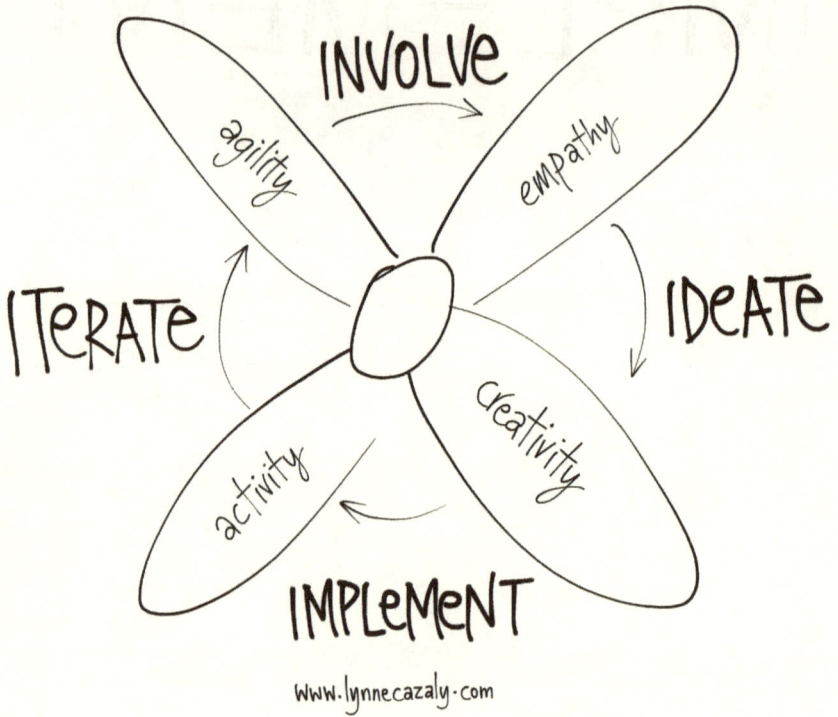

INVOLVE

agility

empathy

ITERATE

IDEATE

creativity

activity

IMPLEMENT

www.lynnecazaly.com

It's in the doing

It's time to test it, try it out, have a go and see what happens. Pick an idea that will solve a customer's problem, challenge or issue and put it into practice.

It really is in the doing.

The release, launch or execution of your idea IS the whole point. Without it, you're wasting effort and limiting possibility. Put your idea out there into the ether. Then watch what happens.

If you don't, it would be like planning a trip or holiday and then not taking it. That's crazy! All that effort and thinking and planning - and then not doing anything with it. Yes you can enjoy dreaming of holiday destinations and looking for quotes and checking out hotel reviews, but one day... make sure you go, ok?

In Peter Cook's book *'The New Rules of Management'* he says that with the evolution of management and leadership, we used to focus on systems and efficiency. Nowadays, we need to be more about putting important projects and pieces of work into practice. He suggests we don't need to be productive first to implement projects, rather we need to implement projects, the things that matter.

This is what it's about; implementing is doing the stuff that matters. When you do the stuff, the implementing, you'll then have things to look at, measure, see and respond to that will lead to greater agility. If you're tinkering with stuff not actually implementing, oh, what a waste. There's nothing to see here.

I used to have a bit of a crush on Australian Jazz Singer Vince Jones. One of his earliest albums *'Watch What Happens'* included a song of the same name, a real jazz classic by Michel Legrand. The lyrics may be about love and letting someone love you, but it's about letting go and then watching what happens when you indeed DO let someone love you. It's the DOING of love, the loving. Watch what happens. When you do the design or the delivery, when you put it into practice, when you launch, release, implement and act, you will indeed be doing and you will have something to iterate and improve on later. Aaaah, just like love!

It may well have been Yoda in the 'Star Wars' franchise who said, 'Do. Or do not. There is no try.' And in the Thought Leaders Business School - where I'm on faculty and spend time advising and mentoring students who are building up their intellectual property and thought leadership - we often say 'You're on the wrong side of a whole lot of work'. That is, you may well have ideas but you've got to test them out. Putting them into the market is part of the work to be done. Working out and scoping out your IP is part of the work to be done. It's in the doing. This is the implementation.

Get something started

Getting it shipped or shared is a mammoth action, there's no doubt about that. As fearful or as worried as you - or your team - may be about what might happen, the other side of action gives us wonderful insights.

Our world revolves on getting started. Think of ignition in a car; modern vehicles today simply have a start/stop button. Earlier makes had a key and you turned the thing 'on'. Fire starts and burns with embers. Spot fires in bushfire season start from a small ember from a neighbouring fire. As dangerous as it is, it is a symbol of how something starts.

In one of my earlier careers I was a radio DJ and enjoyed hunting out cool songs sometimes missed by the mainstream. I think Graham Parker in his song *'Get started, start a fire'* was one of those tunes. He talks about being a bit of a rebel and rule-breaker. Perhaps his version of starting a fire is about being reckless or being controversial, to do something out of the ordinary. And being agile-ish is becoming more popular. It is still new and challenging and different for many people and so to start and implement something you've created with a team in an agile-ish way, then yes, you most likely will be a bit of a rebel. Swimming upstream or against the grain can be exhausting, hard work, but isn't that how all the best changes happen?

Get it done in a hackathon

For many people, teams and units across a business, a breath of fresh air and a jolt of innovation and inspiration is what's needed to press 'reset' and embark on a new financial year or a new project or kick-off a fresh start and implement something.

When businesses like Qantas, nab and SEEK are all about starting something, they get their teams together and hack.

So I'm here to tell ya: the hack is the way to great action and implementation.

Yes, the hack.

Not breaking-into-computers hacking, but rather coming-up-with-ingenious-ideas-for-tricky-problems hacking.

You might have come up with some ideas, potentials, possibilities, but then what?

Known as the 'hack day' or 'hackathon', clued-up businesses are bringing their teams together to identify top talent, reconnect their people, speed up the identification and implementation of ideas and shift up the vibe of the business' culture.

In '3 Reasons your business should host a hackathon' in Inc. Magazine, Dave Kerpen says they are:

1. Bring employees together and increase morale.

2. Reinforce the right values.

3. Leave you with lasting ideas -- and even products.

Too often in team days or dull planning sessions the loudest voices drown out fresh and upcoming idea makers. Or worse, it's a meteor shower of PowerPoint bullet points. And even when ideas are presented, there's a lack of accountability, responsibility or follow through to get things done to see if they'll actually work.

So enter, the hack. A half, one or multi-day hacking event is proving to be a culture shaker, an innovation maker and a rut breaker!

Full on input... and output

Through these creative, collaborative, ingenious and full-on sessions, teams work together to design and deliver something; they create solutions to respond to real customer challenges. That's implementation! Whether that's a new strategy or a new product. With an increasing focus on the customer, businesses of all sizes are seeing this is a swift and clever way to gain a competitive advantage. The hackathon helps develop prototypes that can be put into practice quick smart.

Best of all, you get a taste of agile-ish - a taste of agility and productivity. You get to play with some of the super-human ways of working that leading global businesses who use hacks to their advantage do. Think Google, NASA, Facebook, Salesforce, Uber, eBay, Qantas, Atlassian...

But hey, hackathons don't have to be about technology; it's where they were born, yes, but you can apply hacks to creativity and innovation in almost any aspect of your business, team, unit or industry.

I recently facilitated a hack session at a multi-industry conference; more than 100 people all working on individual projects and tasks but their incredibly productive outputs could only have been achieved in that timeframe using hacking techniques.

Cool companies hack

Big and small companies, teams and projects the world over are seeing the benefits of the hack.

They get teams of people together to work intensively and rapidly to:

- create new products
- focus on customers
- align the team and enterprise
- create solutions to tricky problems
- lift innovative thinking and
- create collaborative environments.

And wait, there's more. I love how hack events help you see how people work under pressure. This type of environment helps you identify top talent, high potentials and high performers who may have been previously hidden, stifled or just uninspired!

Plus it's time to find other ways to break out of those dull ruts and patterns that a team may have fallen victim to over recent times. It's so easy to get comfortable and stay there.

It's also easy to keep talking and planning and talking and planning and meeting and talking and planning and not actually do anything.

Most of all in hackathons, I love seeing teams mixing together - particularly when they're working across silos. People are enjoying the work (because : happiness!) and they're bringing a competitive and cheeky team spirit to the event. The energy is electric and the solutions are often mind blowing!

'Wha?! How did they come up with THAT?' is a phrase that's often heard.

Customer Focus

With a strong customer focus, a hackathon or hack day helps create some big reasons to:

- connect and talk more deeply with customers;
- research and gather information;
- uncover insights; and
- map out customer experiences.

In these insights are genius solutions and ideas that the team can go on to prototype or create during the hack. This is a nice connection to make. Remember right back at the beginning of agile-ish, to INVOLVE the customer, user or client. This is a perfect pre-cursor to a hack; connect with your customers.

Practical ... and Keep Going

Many hackers rave about how practical and productive hackathons are. It's not about talking all day. Yawn! Hack days are about getting sh*t done, doing things. It's about short sprints of activity over the day or days and teams working rapidly, pushing through doubt or procrastination and experiencing a highly productive environment where delivery is everything.

And then with the experience of the hack, teams take hacking elements back to their workplace and workspace and find they're able to generate innovative ideas and work productively by applying the same, again and again.

One team I worked with recently continued using their 'Hack Pack': it's a collection of practices I run during a hack day. When they want to re-live the creativity, productivity and collaboration experience of the hackathon in their everyday work, they simply choose a technique from the *Hack Pack* ... and go!

7 things

Now, before you go all crazy and book a venue and invite everyone to hack together, think about these seven things first (from one of my blogs about hackathons):

1. **Focus:** why are we going to hack and what might the theme be?
2. **Hackers:** who's in? Who wants to come, needs to be there or would benefit from the lift of the hack?
3. **Schedule:** what's going to happen when on the day? What's the schedule of things?
4. **Process:** how are you going to hack? What will you do when? Who will facilitate it for you?
5. **Celebrate:** how will you cheer on the ideas, outputs and progress the hackers make throughout the day?
6. **Implement:** how will you bring the prototypes you create to fruition and put them into practice beyond the hack?
7. Integrate: how will you weave the learnings from the event into your culture for ongoing benefits, return on investment and overall hacking goodness?

Leading companies and businesses across so many industries (beyond technology) are learning that today's challenges need new ways of thinking, acting and working. They're looking for better ways to drive creativity and ingenuity - yet all the while still solving problems and challenges. Oh and let's maintain or strengthen our competitive advantage at the same time!

When you need to get all of that done, where there's a hack ... there is most certainly a way!

Failure is an option

There's plenty of talk in business today about failing, failing fast, failing forward and my favourite, failing fast *and* failing often.

The problem is, plenty of those businesses don't have anything in place that actually supports a risky endeavor nor a process to review and learn from the failure.

Most often I see leaders or conference speakers saying *'we need to fail fast'* yet they don't provide any processes or structure within which to test, experiment, try... and then fail... and most importantly, learn from it. No wonder everyone keeps playing excruciatingly safe!

Low risk, no fail, no dent in career path, no look bad, no get into trouble and no lose annual bonus.

Back in 2011, *Harvard Business Review* released *'The Failure Issue'* and dealt with all things f-word.

Of some of the different types of failure to think and know about, my ears and eyes pricked up at the concept (or practicality of) *'Intelligent Failure'*. As author, Amy Edmonson explains, these failures are at the frontier:

'Failures in this category can rightly be considered 'good', because they provide valuable new knowledge that can help an organization leap ahead of the competition and ensure its future growth—which is why the Duke University professor of management Sim Sitkin calls them intelligent failures. They occur when experimentation is necessary: when answers are not knowable in advance because this exact situation hasn't been encountered before and perhaps never will be again. Discovering new drugs, creating a radically new business, designing an innovative product, and testing customer reactions in a brand-new market are tasks that require intelligent failures.'

Oh this is so smart, hey?

The creation and support of this type of learning culture helps us examine 'what happened', rather than 'who stuffed up?'

Plus, if we're to respond, adapt and move quickly, we have to experiment. As all great scientists, discoverers, explorers and first movers know, the quicker we fail, the sooner we will have the opportunity to learn something.

True, failing doesn't feel good but if you set up for it in the first place, you'll be more likely to create a 'lab' experience your team will want to play in rather than a 'courtroom' experience they will try and avoid at all costs.

Testing, trying and seeing what happened ...is the bomb.

Oh and don't go dressing things up as a long-suffering, eons-in-the-making 'pilot' and making out it's some kind of experiment designed to learn and fail fast. Too often we have our hands tightly gripped around all of the elements of a pilot, saying it's an experiment but trying at every point to not let it fall, fail or stumble.

Standout organisations don't just put the detective to work analyzing failures or looking to blame, point fingers or reprimand people. Rather they set out to deliberately create experiments and implement things specifically for learning and testing and trying and... innovating.

So get planning a hack day... heck, even a hack two hours is better than not hacking at all!

If you can't get sign off for a bigger hacking event, run an informal one in your team or area. Lots of businesses do them on the weekend. You don't have to do it every weekend; just one, a Saturday morning or a Sunday afternoon. Not everyone has to come. Careful what you might be thinking or resisting here. I've worked with incredible teams who've had hundreds of people show up on a weekend to work on exhilarating, creative and productive stuff. It's electrifying. Such passion, commitment and energy from people who supposedly 'can't come in on the weekend because the kids play soccer.' Incredibly swift arrangements soon got made with the grandparents to get the kids to soccer that day. ;-)

If you can't proceed with hacking the team, then hack yourself. Run a small hack session on yourself, your work, the stuff you do for clients, consumers and customers.

It is impossible to live
without failing at something,
unless you live so cautiously
that you might as well not
lived at all.

In which case, you've failed
by default.

- JK Rowling

Lynne Cazaly

ITERATE

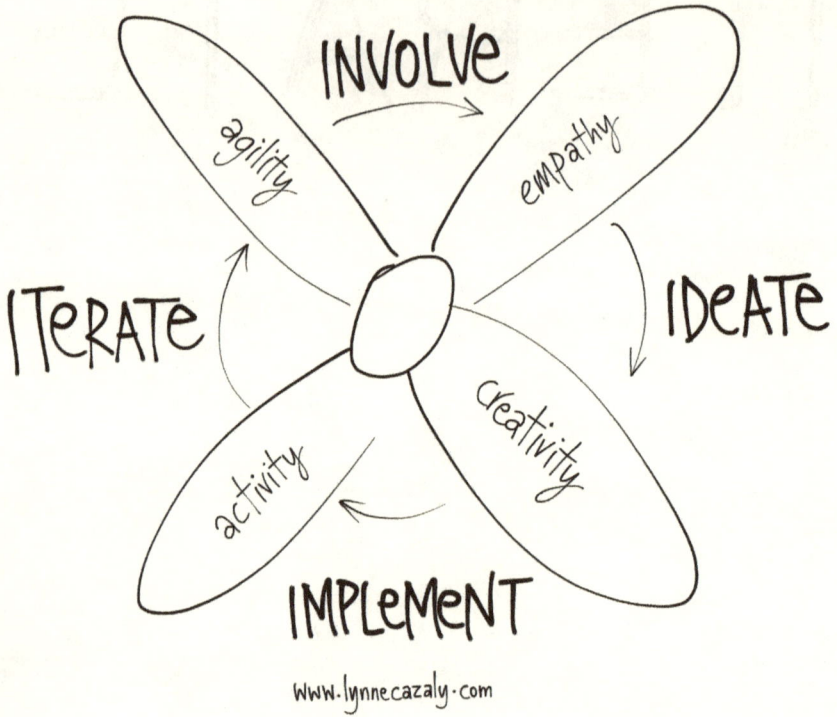

INVOLVE

agility

empathy

ITERATE

IDEATE

creativity

activity

IMPLEMENT

www.lynnecazaly.com

Have another go

Iterate means to repeat, redo or go over, to do again. Once it's done, it's kind of not done. Well it's done, but there is opportunity for tweaking, improvement, changing and adding. All the while adding more or better value or doing a better job than the first cut or first version.

So go again. Have another go. Make some changes and do it again. See what happens. Then go again. Release another version. And another.

Put the 'Changes Welcome' mat out

I love those doormats at people's front doors that say things like:

- 'Oh no not you again'
- 'I am not a doormat'
- 'The neighbours have better stuff'.

But perhaps the most common doormat simply says 'Welcome'. It's saying 'yes' and 'hello' and 'come on in... you're safe here'. And in organisations going through change, transformation, evolution, you most certainly need a mat – one that says 'Changes Welcome'.

So do you put the welcome mat out during change or are you running off down a path with the gate locked behind you? Welcoming changes is a philosophy of agile. Software developers being agile welcome changes because they are on a path of iterating and editing and reviewing and releasing changed and improved versions of software, website, app or technology. Even if it's later in the process, changes, comments, and responses are welcome. That means what they're creating will be more useful, more suitable.

Welcome changes from customers, clients and end users, no matter what stage of the process of design, development, delivery or sale of your thing, product, change, transformation or service.

This is about acceptance, flexibility and adaptability. It's this input that keeps people engaged in what you're doing and makes what you're doing more tailored to the people who are using it. When changes come to you whether that be today, tomorrow or next week, note how you respond. Are you welcoming or are you locking yourself away from them.

Beyond version one

The stories of scientists, explorers and inventors tend to have a common theme - don't give up. It's a message of *'keep going, you've not done your best work yet or you've not found the thing yet... there is still more experimenting and testing to do.'* The same applies in having an agile-ish approach or mindset.

There is a Russian idiom that says (in a modern spelling) ПЕРВЫЙ БЛИН КОМОМ, which means 'the first pancake is always a lumpy one'. When you've created the batter and whipped it up and you pour it into the pan, the pan isn't perhaps at optimum heat yet or the spatula isn't warmed up or the pan hasn't even had the pancake mixture on it yet. The first one isn't going to be perfect. Later ones will look much better. So we need to allow for some lumps in things. This applies to anything you're putting an agile-ish mindset to. Don't stop at version one, there is better to come. Perfection doesn't come on the first attempt - you'll have to go again, and again. And again.

If you have a look at the version of any app you're using on your smart phone or the version of a software application on your desktop you'll find that it isn't Version 1. Even new apps will have gone through a few versions, perhaps 1.456 or 2.32 or 10.3.4.56 or some other numbering system that lets the creators know what they're up to.

Looking at the Evernote app I use, it's up to Version 8.6.358974.

You're using products, technology and services every day that have been through so many iterations and changes. It's time to let go of those expectations of perfection.

Rather, go for iteration.

It's been suggested that Amazon - fully loaded with apps and software brimming from every pore - releases updates every 11 seconds. Yep. Another update issued while you were reading this sentence. They are constantly and continually updating and iterating, improving and reissuing. This is agile-ish. And they are most agile.

No athlete worth their medal or personal best would stop at their first attempt. Russian-born Australian pole-vaulter Tatiana Grigorieva was training for the Olympics in Sydney, Australia back in the late 1990s in readiness for the 2000 Olympics. She migrated to Australia from Russia in 1997 and took up the sport of pole vaulting. Fearless and bold woman. Love it.

While many athletes enjoy some natural abilities or affinities for sports, they're never so perfect that it takes them just one attempt or in Grigorieva's case, one jump. Nope. They train, they test, they improve and they adjust tiny, minute aspects of their training and performance. With the pole vault, that scary run towards an indentation or 'the box' in the track and then that high lift as they hurl themselves skyward on a bent pole to fully extend and reach over the high bar, only to plummet back down to earth, to land on the soft mat on their back. Yikes! Iteration is a constant. It's part of the process of improvement. The precision comes from repeated actions and tweaking the tiny elements of those actions.

Any novice golfer would also know this; hold your head still, shift the hips, lift the heel but don't twist, cock the wrists and downward swing, hips leading, keep the club face and angle steady, follow through and keep your head down. So many elements to one swing that get repeated and repeated, tweaked and adjusted.

If iteration is the only thing you get from agile-ish, I'd be a happy person.

Improvement is always possible

The evolution and improvement of your idea, product or thing is a natural motivation and progression. I don't think you should fight it. Be willing – and encouraging -- for it to get better. Even actors and directors work on second, third and 15th takes. Perhaps a 'mis-take' is just that; another go at something. Through the repetition we're able to improve, willing to improve, wanting to improve and make better. It must be part of the human condition.

The classic Marcus Aurelius quote: *'All things are in the act of change; thou thyself in ceaseless transformation and partial decay, and the whole universe with thee.'*

We are all changing, all of us, everything, always.

Your product, service, idea, project, too will change. Why not be open to the change as being an improvement in value, an iteration, an evolution.

This type of mindset gets you into a space of incredible possibilities.

Close the loop and let them know

This may sound simple and straightforward or obvious but so often we get caught up in the next best thing, the next bright shiny object or the next distraction that closing the loop gets forgotten about. We forget to reconnect with those who helped us at the start; or we forget to communicate and advise or inform others of what's going on as a result of their input.

Here is the opportunity to make it part of 'how we do things around here'. We iterate. And we let people know about it.

Invite them back to participate and contribute again.

Find out what's changed for them -- because it can change for you too.

And by keeping the communication going from when you opened it up by asking and involving people, you set up opportunities for ongoing improvement, more iterations and then around you go... more involvement.

Keep on iterating

Let people know this is a first cut or the first version or whatever version number you're up to.

Invite them to comment and provide input to it.

Don't make it look too 'perfect'. Straight lines, perfect boxes and hours spent on PowerPoint documents don't invite comment or input.

I think we can all be less in love with the expectation of perfection. Let's be more into iteration.

Close the loop and let them know how you've incorporated their input into the next version.

Share the next version with them.

And the next.

And the next.

Keep in touch.

Lynne Cazaly

BUILD A MOVEMENT

Agile-ish

Working together

Don't try this stuff alone; well, certainly adjust your own mindset before attempting to influence others, but it will be mighty helpful to have a team, tribe and movement around you.

Simon Sinek says *a movement starts with a clear vision of a world different than the one we live in today*.

There's so much reading on change for leaders available in the market today. Whether the wildly successful *'Immunity to Change'*, the practical *'Made to Stick'* from Dan and Chip Heath or the timeless *'Leading Change'* of John Kotter.

Lisa Laskow Lahey and Robert Kegan, authors of *'Immunity to Change'* say, *'courage involves the ability to take action and carry on even when we are afraid.'* There may well be times during change, transformation and breaking new ground that you are afraid.

There is much to be learned from how social and community (and political) movements build and grow and shift and transform; how people are enrolled and how others rise to advocate and then enrol others. It's less multi-level marketing, more tribal, more willing, more drive and desire to be a part of; less conscription or prescription.

In the *Harvard Business Review* article (by Sarah A Soule and Bryan Walker) *'Changing Company Culture Requires a Movement, Not a Mandate'* it's stated that:

'Culture change can't be achieved through top-down mandate. It lives in the collective hearts and habits of people and their shared perception of "how things are done around here." Someone with authority can demand compliance, but they can't dictate optimism, trust, conviction, or creativity. ... the most significant change often comes through social movements, and that despite the differences between private enterprises and society, leaders can learn from how these initiators engage and mobilize the masses to institutionalize new societal norms.'

As they go on to explain in the article, movements start with emotion rather than what we often think might be the 'call to action' or a call to arms.

It's where there might be a dissatisfaction with the status quo or a realisation that the way things are is not the way they need to be; perhaps that the way things are won't help us in the future - things *will* need to be different.

Discontent rises and once there is a positive voice pointing (and painting) a clear vision of the possible future and a path forward - in the words of late 1970's disco band McFadden and Whitehead *'Ain't no stopping us now'*.

> *Ain't No Stoppin Us Now!*
> *We're on the move!*
> *Ain't No Stoppin Us Now!*
> *We've got the groove!*

The groove. The groove as a dance move; the groove as an analogue record was made of. Once you're in it, it's so much easier. Friction is reduced and the journey is smoother.

And relax because to get started, you don't need a cast of thousands. Plenty of movements start small, way small, petite even. A group of passionate people celebrating a few small wins and you're on your way. I think this is why the experimentation part of being agile-ish is so powerful.

It helps:

- build confidence among the team;
- attract positive attention (*hey, they're doing cool stuff*); and
- learn swiftly so you can adapt and improve on the next round or next release.

The reward of the celebration is a wonderful thing! Those non-believers who might be watching from afar (or within) will be drawn to what you're celebrating and what you're changing, as small as it might be. This goes a long way to helping engage those who may have doubted or dissed what you're working on.

You can't just talk about the need for change.

I see and hear many change leaders trying to do this; bleating louder about why this change is needed. The phrase 'create the urgency' makes me break out in a sweat. It's such a clichéd and manipulative term to try and push people towards why they *should* get on board, but that's a motivation that will be short lived. There's little substance behind it. Where's the desire and responsibility to change? The deep wanting or will? Where's the BIG meaning behind this?

Further in that *Harvard Business Review* article the authors further highlight that we shouldn't point out the end shift we're looking for, but rather the behaviours we'd like to see. In the case of agile-ish, that might mean being closer to customers, coming up with ideas, testing out our ideas, running experiments, risking failure, learning from the experiments, putting things out there, trying again, improving and evolving, iterating... and continuing on with it all again.

Symbols of change

Make sure you help people see that things are underway and there is change afoot. A lot of digital transformation is happening behind computer screens and via people staring at those screens. That may look no different whether it's a team in technology, a team in finance, the team at reception, or the team in marketing.

As the wonderful Soule and Walker article in *Harvard Business Review* says:

'Embrace symbols. Movement makers are experts at constructing and deploying symbols and costumes that simultaneously create a feeling of solidarity and demarcate who they are and what they stand for to the outside world. Symbols and costumes of solidarity help define the boundary between "us" and "them" for movements. These symbols can be as simple as a T-shirt, bumper sticker, or button supporting a general cause, or as elaborate as the giant puppets we often see used in protest events.'

They refer to older, last century ways of leading and thinking, advising us to remember, *'it's easy to overuse one's authority in the hopes of accelerating transformation.'*

I think you need to apply pressure and then let go. Let people try it out and experience and learn more about the change. Push? No.

When the sh*t hits the fan

A lot of people won't like the changes and transformations you're making no matter whether it's agile-ish or not. For many people you'll look like you're changing things 180 degrees, or more. They'll feel tumble-dried and inverted! Soule and Walker say:

> 'It's also easy for an enterprise leader to shy away from organizational friction. Harmony is generally a preferred state, after all. And the success of an organizational transition is often judged by its seamlessness.'

As with all good change and transformation, some friction and unrest is good; it's causing discomfort and transition after all. Imagine if there was silence? Perhaps the change ain't big enough. Or maybe no one is listening!

When I'm facilitating workshops and sessions with teams - and while I don't particularly like conflict - it's the space or place where some of the best work and transformation can occur. That is, if you delve a little deeper, take some time to understand what's causing the conflict, you can uncover some wonderful things and make great progress, getting around or through obstacles and barriers that have previously been impassable.

A coalition of the new

Daily we see the power of networks and influence in our communities and workplaces. Those who are making changes via movements are great coalition builders and they're able to bring people together. It's something I've often admired; how these collaborative and influential people are able to bring seemingly disconnected views together to create a larger group that's now aligned in purpose and direction.

Janine Garner in her book *'It's Who You Know: How a network of 12 people can fast-track your success'* validates this further explaining that we have key people who - when around us - help keep us focused to get the right stuff done. Rather than going for a quantity of people in your network, make sure you have the people around you who will support you, cheer you and guide you towards the agile-ish success you've got your sights set on.

The top four people Garner suggests you need in your midst are:

1. Promoters

These are your personal cheerleaders. They never give up and they dream big with you. Garner says they *'pull you towards your future dreams, make noise about possibilities, spend time with you to explore how you're going to achieve your goals and inspire you.'* This is ideal for agile-ish journeys. Don't do this thing alone. Make sure you have a promoter – or three – on your team!

2. Pit-crew

The right crew will help you through the tough days, keeping you mentally tough and balanced. Garner says, *'They add stamina, help to navigate complexities and lift you up after setbacks; they help you learn from mistakes and push you on.'*

A-ha, also helpful in agile-ish worlds. Especially when things haven't gone so well, you'll need to identify the learnings and insights so you can make the next cycle and next iteration an experience of continuous experimentation and improvement.

3. Teachers

Teachers push us. They can open doors and see things in different ways. These are your coaches and mentors; the people who've been there and done it and can help you through on a path of least resistance. Tap into the wide global network of agilists who will share their journeys and experiences with you.

4. Butt-kickers

'Love them or hate them,' says Garner, *'we all need butt-kickers. They are the masters of delivery. They listen to your dreams and accelerate your goals, pushing you to do more and holding you accountable for all your actions – and then some.'* So who's on your team through this journey?

Rather than fighting it out with the non-supporters, nay sayers and white ant-ers, get a greater coalition of supporters behind you. Any leader of a movement identifies their allies - not that it needs to be war-like - but people on your side of the fence, or in your realm of thinking who are vital to help initiate change, progress... and be successful.

'The Courage to Be Disliked' by Fumitake Koga and Ichiro Kishimi really hits on the topic of perhaps having to go it alone at some point.

'Someone has to start. Other people might not be cooperative, but that is not connected to you. My advice is this: You should start. With no regard to whether others are cooperative or not.'

Lessons from Steve

Steve Denning, author, and one of the worlds leading thinkers – who presents at many an agile conference – recently reported on some insights from a project he was involved in. The Learning Consortium's focus of work was to discover what is actually happening in agile circles.

Denning suggests there is a fair bit of uncertainty - not just in the world - but in what people are doing in agile.

To get some hard and fast information, the Learning Consortium conducted studies and visits and gathered information on what was going down!

Sponsored by the *Scrum Alliance*, the program followed 11 firms - of the likes of Microsoft, Ericsson, Menlo Innovations and Riot Games – and found that agile practices have spread beyond software and into mainstream management.

They also found that large firms have learned how to become agile at scale and the management practices of agile are successfully handling complexity as well as being highly reliable and durable.

In a beautiful summary of the lessons learned from the Learning Consortium's work, Denning presented on *'How to make the whole organisation agile'* at a conference in Australia in 2016.

The 12 lessons were:

1. Acquiring the mindset can take time

2. Implementing takes time

3. Firms are at different places on the journey

4. All the journeys involved setbacks

5. Adapt practices to fit

6. The practices are durable and fragile

7. It can create a passionate workforce

8. The transition is happening

9. It's not about being digital

10. It's not about giving up control

11. You need to get started

12. The journey never ends - you never arrive.

Thanks Steve. I love your work!

Thoroughly modern

The practice of agile is a teenager - it's about 15 years old.

There's even a Modern Agile movement, spearheaded by Joshua Kerievsky that's gaining traction and interest. The thinking here is that over the past 15 years, many organisations have found even more simpler ways to be agile.

The principles of Modern Agile are:

- Make people awesome
- Make safety a prerequisite
- Experiment and learn rapidly
- Deliver value continuously.

I love working with leadership teams and exploring these four principles in discussions, debate, storytelling and reflection.

Whatever you say it is or isn't, agile is about responding and adapting so it makes sense that those who have an agile mindset might also be keen on making changes and adaptations to the practices and methods of agile itself!

Like any field of expertise there are always discussions and debates about which is the best approach, when, where and why.

There's certainly plenty of debate at agile conferences and in social media discussion group. This diversity is healthy for a field of interest or endeavour; it's the thing that helps it grow and progress. Medicine would be nothing without this kind of debate and progression, neither would aviation, design, engineering or zoology for that matter!

Start with you

Start with you, your mindset, your way of thinking and your way of working... and then go from there.

There are said to be more than 70 different practices under the bigger agile umbrella and that umbrella has probably gathered a few other sorts who want to connect, grow or prosper alongside it!

When a fellow Australian colleague, Craig Smith was presenting on 40 of these agile methods at a conference a while ago, I wrote them all down as he rapidly talked through them. It's not just a list but a whole page! You'll find a visual below.

If you're wondering what Large Scale Scrum, Beyond Budgeting, Mob Programming or TDD is ... press your Google button to learn more! You'll find whole communities devoted to many of these methods so you can go as deep as you like to learn more and be even more agile-ish.

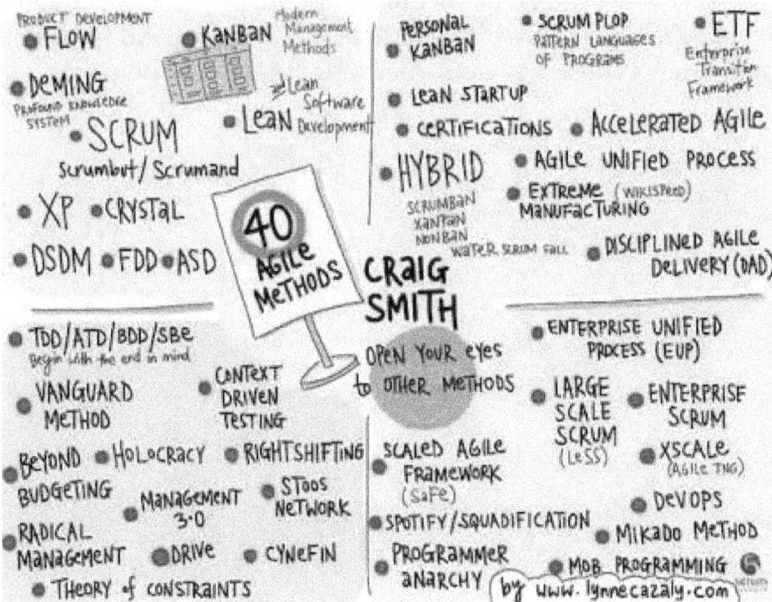

I can't not mention Scrum here. It's an *'agile framework for completing complex projects'*, so says the *Scrum Alliance*. Yes it may have a metaphorical connection to the rugby scrum but it's also made up of some wonderfully clear and simple rituals or techniques that many people start trying out to get a taste of what agile could be like. Scrum might have started in software development but it's adopted in many different fields and businesses now.

And Scrum Founder, Dr Jeff Sutherland's book *'Scrum: The Art of doing twice the work in half the time'* is a wonderful read!

Another favourite is Jurgen Appelo's *'Management 3.0'* movement. The old ways of management are gone; we're now in a world where businesses and teams can work in ways that deliver more, better... and the people in those teams are happier than ever.

Remember agile is about how you think, and it's about delivering value to customers more efficiently.

Agile is more than a cliché, more than just a phrase of *'we need to be more agile'*. In fact we all need to adapt and respond like never before; some of these agile-ish methods might just help you and your clients do that. And then you can play with them, adapt them and shape them to fit.

Go you! Be agile. Ish.

People take the longest possible paths, digress to numerous dead ends, and make all kinds of mistakes.

Then historians come along and write summaries of this messy, nonlinear process and make it appear like a simple, straight line.

- Dean Kamen

Agile-ish

REFERENCES & READING

Agile Manifesto. Manifesto for Agile Software Development. *Manifesto for Agile Software Development*, agilemanifesto.org/

Agile HR Manifesto. Principles behind the Agile HR Manifesto. *Manifesto for Agile HR Development*, www.agilehrmanifesto.org/principles-behind-the-hr-manifesto.

Appelo, Jurgen. *Management 3.0: Leading Agile Developers, Developing Agile Leaders.* 1st ed., Addison-Wesley, 2011.

Catmull, Ed and Wallace, Amy. '*Creativity Inc: Overcoming the unseen forces that stand in the way of true inspiration',* 2014. Bantam Press.

Cockburn, Alistair. "The Heart of Agile." *The Heart of Agile | Rediscovering The Heart and Spirit of Agile*, Alistair Cockburn, 24 Mar. 2015, heartofagile.com/.

Bariso, Justin. "Elon Musk Takes Customer Complaint on Twitter From Idea to Execution in 6 Days." *Inc*, 9 Jan. 2017, www.inc.com/justin-bariso/elon-musk-takes-customer-complaint-on-twitter-from-idea-to-execution-in-6-days.html.

Bregman, Peter. *Four Seconds: All The Time You Need To Replace Counter-Productive Habits With Ones That Really Work*. New York, NY, HarperOne, an imprint of HarperCollins Publishers, 2016.

Briggs, Sara. "Agile Based Learning: What Is It and How Can It Change Education?" *InformED*, 22 Feb. 2014, www.opencolleges.edu.au/informed/features/agile-based-learning-what-is-it-and-how-can-it-change-education/.

Collister, Patrick. *How to use innovation and creativity in the workplace.* Pan Macmillian 2017

Cook, Peter. *The New Rules of Management: How to Revolutionise Productivity, Innovation and Engagement by Implementing Projects That Matter.* John Wiley and Sons Australia, Ltd., 2013.

De La Maza, Michael, and David Benz. *Why Agile Works: The Values Behind The Results*. www.infoq.com/resource/minibooks/why-agile-works/en/pdf/InfoQ-Why-Agile-Works-Mini-book.pdf.

Denning, Steve, et al. "Exploring Whether Agile is Still Agile." InfoQ, 5 December. 2016, www.infoq.com/podcasts/leading-minds.

Denning, Steve. "Learning Consortium For The Creative Economy Is Launched." Forbes, 21 April. 2015, www.forbes.com/sites/stevedenning/2015/04/21/learning-consortium-for-the-creative-economy-is-launched/#2a9c99d91ae0.

Denning, Steve. "Learning Consortium For The Creative Economy." Forbes, 2 November. 2015, www.forbes.com/sites/stevedenning/2015/11/02/drucker-forum-2015-tackles-the-creative-economy/#7669e86b1697.

Edmonson, Amy C. "Strategies for Learning from Failure." *Harvard Business Review,* hbr.org/2011/04/strategies-for-learning-from-failure?referral=03758&cm_vc=rr_item_page.top_right.

Falcone, John. "7 Reasons Why Some Corporations Hate Agile Methodologies." *The Agile Times,* The Agile Times, 8 September. 2015, theagiletimes.com/7-reasons-why-some-corporations-hate-agile-methodologies/.

Fyffe, Steve, and Karen Lee. "How Design Thinking Improves the Creative Process." *Insights by Stanford Business,* Stanford Graduate School of Business, 19 January. 2016, www.gsb.stanford.edu/insights/how-design-thinking-improves-creative-process.

Garner, Janine. *It's Who You Know: How a Network of 12 Key People Can Fast-Track Your Success.* Wiley, 2017.

Garton, Eric and Noble, Andy. *'How to make agile work for the C-Suite'* Harvard Bsuiness Review July 19, 2017. https://hbr.org/2017/07/how-to-make-agile-work-for-the-c-suite

Godin, Seth. *Tribes: We Need You to Lead Us.* New York, Portfolio, 2008.

Gower, Bob. *Agile Business: A Leader's Guide to Harnessing Complexity.* Rally Software, 2013.

Hamel, Gary, and Michelle Zanini. "Assessment: Do You Know How Bureaucratic Your Organization Is?" *Harvard Business Review,* 16 May 2017, hbr.org/2017/05/assessment-do-you-know-how-bureaucratic-your-organization-is.

Hastie, Shane, and Jenni Jepsen. "Neuroscience Behind Why Agile Works." *InfoQ,* C4Media Inc., 5 May 2015, www.infoq.com/interviews/jepsen-why-agile-works.

Johnson, Stephen Scott. *Emergent: Ignite Purpose, Transform Culture, Make Change Stick.* John Wiley and Sons Australia, Ltd., 2017.

Johnson, Steven. *Emergent.* 2017, www.stephenscottjohnson.com/wp-content/uploads/2016/06/Emergent_The-Future-of-Culture-2016.pdf.

Judkins, Rod. *Ideas Are Your Only Currency*. Hodder & Stoughton, 2017.

Kapoor, Bharat, et al. "How GE Appliances Built an Innovation Lab to Rapidly Prototype Products." *Harvard Business Review*, 18 July 2017, hbr.org/2017/07/how-ge-built-an-innovation-lab-to-rapidly-prototype-appliances.

Kerpen, Dave. "3 Reasons why your business should host a hackathon". *Inc Magazine*. June 19, 2015.

Kishimi, Ichiro and Fumitake Koga. *Courage to be Disliked: How to Free Yourself, Change Your Life and Achieve Real Happiness*. Allen & Unwin, 2017

Knapp, Jake, et al. *Sprint: How to Solve Big Problems and Test New Ideas in Just Five Days*. Simon & Schuster , 2016.

Kolko, John. *Well-Designed: How to Use Empathy to Create Products People Love*. Harvard Business Review Press, 2014

Kolko, Jon. "Design Thinking Comes of Age." *Harvard Business Review,* hbr.org/2015/09/design-thinking-comes-of-age.

Lindstrom, Martin. *Small Data: The Tiny Clues That Uncover Huge Trends*. St. Martin's Press, 2016.

Lyons, Dan. "How to Master Change." *Fortune*, 11 Nov. 2016, fortune.com/2016/11/11/nvidia-ai-self-driving-cars/.

McGeorge, Donna. "Cultural Change?! It's not HR's job!!!" *LinkedIn*, 6 April. 2015, www.linkedin.com/pulse/cultural-change-its-hrs-job-donna-mcgeorge

McQueen, Michael. *Momentum: How to Build It, Keep It or Get It Back*. Wiley, 2016.

Patel, Deep. "10 Ways Leaders Can Better Connect With Their Customers." *Forbes*, 22 June 2017, www.forbes.com/sites/deeppatel/2017/06/22/10-ways-leaders-can-better-connect-with-their-customers/#4e06aa407b02.

Port, Michael, and Elizabeth Marshall. *The Contrarian Effect: Why It Pays (Big) to Take Typical Sales Advice and Do the Opposite*. John Wiley & Sons 2008.

Sahota, Michael. "WHY Agile?" Workshop." *Agilitrix | Helping You Grow Your Organization*, 6 June 2014, agilitrix.com/2014/06/agile-is-not-the-goal-workshop/.

Scrum Alliance. 'Learn About Scrum' *Scrum Alliance,* www.scrumalliance.org/why-scrum.

Sutherland, Jeff. *Scrum: The Art of Doing Twice the Work in Half the Time.* Crown Business, 2014

Ting, Deanna, and Frits Van Paasschen. "Interview: Ex-Starwood CEO on the Essentials to Disrupting Any Industry." *Skift*, 25 January 2017, skift.com/2017/01/25/interview-ex-starwood-ceo-on-7-ingredients-to-being-a-disruptor/.

Walker, Bryan, and Sarah A Soule. "Changing Company Culture Requires a Movement, Not a Mandate." *Harvard Business Review,* 20 June 2017, hbr.org/2017/06/changing-company-culture-requires-a-movement-not-a-mandate.

World Economic Forum. "Skills for Your Future." *World Economic Forum,* www.weforum.org/focus/skills-for-your-future.

About Lynne Cazaly

Lynne Cazaly is an international keynote speaker, author and mentor. She's known for her humour, straight talk and highly practical skills and insights.

She is the author of five books:

- *Agile-ish: How to create a culture of agility*
- *Leader as Facilitator: How to engage, inspire and get work done*
- *Making Sense: A Handbook for the Future of Work*
- *Create Change: How to apply innovation in an era of uncertainty, and*
- *Visual Mojo: How to capture thinking, convey information and collaborate using visuals.*

She works with executives, senior leaders and project teams on their major change and transformation projects. She helps people distil their thinking, apply ideas and innovation and boost the engagement levels and collaboration effectiveness of teams.

Lynne is an experienced board director and chair. She is a partner with Thought Leaders Global and a Mentor on the Faculty of Thought Leaders Business School.

She lives in Australia in Melbourne with her husband Michael and enjoys hopping on a plane to travel, speak, train and connect with people. As a mad #avgeek, she loves all things aviation, air traffic control, runways and airports!

See more at www.lynnecazaly.com

✶ www.lynnecazaly.com

Lynne Cazaly

Programs, Keynotes and Workshops

Lynne Cazaly's presentations and workshops focus on topics like:

- Working Together and Collaboration
- A Culture of Agility
- Sensemaking: The #1 Capability for a World of Uncertainty
- Facilitation and Group Work
- Creativity and Innovation
- Thought Leadership: Building your team of corporate entrepreneurs

Lynne Cazaly

✶ www.lynnecazaly.com

www.ingramcontent.com/pod-product-compliance
Lightning Source LLC
Chambersburg PA
CBHW031930190326
41519CB00007B/475